Remember a time when you and your mate
weren't too tired for romance?

According to Ellen Kreidman, rekindling the spark
begins by acknowledging three core principles:

★ If you don't have an affair with your mate, you
   risk the possibility that someone else will.

★ The best gift you can ever give your children is a
   loving and lasting relationship with each other.

★ The happiest, most well-adjusted children come
   from a home in which the parents love each other.

Is There Sex After Kids? teaches you how to put the
sizzle of courtship back in your marriage, have your
emotional and sexual needs met, and rediscover the
passion that brought you together.

IS THERE SEX AFTER KIDS?

ELLEN KREIDMAN

(published in hardcover as *How Can We Light a Fire When the Kids Are Driving Us Crazy?*)

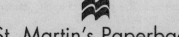

St. Martin's Paperbacks

Published in hardcover as *How Can We Light a Fire When the Kids Are Driving Us Crazy?*

Published by arrangement with Villard Books.

IS THERE SEX AFTER KIDS?

Library of Congress Catalog Card Number: 93-14740

ISBN: 0-312-95866-8

Printed in the United States of America

Villard hardcover edition / September 1993
St. Martin's Paperbacks edition / June 1996

St. Martin's Paperbacks are published by St. Martin's Press, 175 Fifth Avenue, New York, NY 10010.

10 9 8 7 6 5 4 3 2 1

This book is dedicated to my husband, Steve. I love sharing life with you—not just the big, memorable occasions with music and candlelight, but all the ordinary moments that make up our lives as well. Together, we have raised three wonderful children. Every day I spend with you is precious to me and gives me even more reasons to love you. Whenever I've needed you, I've found your arms around me. Whenever I've leaned on you, I've felt your strength.

ACKNOWLEDGMENTS

I will be forever grateful to the following people in my life who have given me their support and encouragement.

To my children, Tara, Tiffany, and Jason, who brighten every day of my life.

To Diane Reverand, my brilliant and intuitive editor, for her work in bringing this book to completion.

To Sandra Caton, whose creative talents and endless hours of dedication helped shape my manuscript.

To Frankie Wright, whose friendship, encouragement, and support have meant a great deal to me.

To my brother, Harvey Wolf, for his wonderful sense of humor and the ability to brighten some very dreary days.

I also owe a great deal to the following wonderful people: Alfred Wolf; Susan, Matthew, and Allison Wolf; Barbara and Dale Vaughan; Robert Schuster; Dr. Mitchell Karlan; Dr. Vicki Hufnagel; Sue Winn; and Dr. Neil Barth and his entire staff.

Finally, I extend a special thanks to each and every one of the graduates of "Light His Fire" and "Light Her Fire" who shared their experiences as parents with me. Without them, this book could not have been written.

A NOTE FROM THE AUTHOR

Most couples have a difficult time keeping romance, passion, excitement, and communication alive in their relationships. In 1981, in El Toro, California, I took a very small step toward helping couples whose relationships had gone stale in my own community. I rented a small office on a month-to-month basis, furnished it classroom style, and began my first formal class of "Light His Fire" for women. One year later, I organized the class for men and began teaching "Light Her Fire."

In 1989, my first book, *Light His Fire: How to Keep Your Man Passionately and Hopelessly in Love with You*, was published. One year later, *Light Her Fire: How to Ignite Passion and Excitement in the Woman You Love* followed. Both books gave me the opportunity to appear on TV and radio, where I could share my thoughts and ideas with a national audience.

After teaching my classes myself for fifteen years, today both classes are being taught throughout the United States and in other parts of the world by dedicated instructors who have been given special training by me. I still spend a great deal of time lecturing to thousands of men and women who want more fulfilling and rewarding relationships.

The game How to Host a Romantic Evening, by Decipher, based on my books, provides couples with hours of entertainment and intimacy, and I've produced an audiocassette program for those who find it geographically impossible to attend a live presentation.

All of these efforts are designed to work together to achieve one ultimate goal: to strengthen the love, romance, excitement, and communication between two people.

SUCCESS STORIES

I am constantly amazed at the number of people who have taken the time to write to me to tell me about the wonderful changes my books, *Light His Fire* and *Light Her Fire*, brought to their lives. What I've learned from thousands of letters from all over the world is that no matter how different we may appear to others, underneath we all have the same need to be loved, appreciated, and cherished. I cried tears of joy with a woman from Iowa and rejoiced with a man whose home was Hong Kong. I learned that a woman in Holland was as profoundly affected as a woman in Maine; and a man from Canada had the same response to my book as a man in New Mexico.

There are no words to describe how wonderful I feel to know that my books have had such a positive impact on so many people's lives. Let me share just a few of the many success stories sent to me by my readers.

WHO SAYS MEN CAN'T CHANGE?

Here is a letter from "Smooth Larry"—the nickname his girlfriend gave him:

I'm a forty-six-year-old divorced male. I recently read your book, *Light Her Fire*. If I could have had my hands on that book ten years ago, I probably would not be divorced today. Your book seemed to describe my life in detail. There was no great romance between my mother and father and there certainly was no display of affection for anyone in the family by anyone else. Each individual was selfish and I was no exception. This attitude obviously carried over into my marriage and while it was not a completely unpleasant marriage it was very dull. You already know all the reasons. They are scattered throughout your book. By the way, I finished the book in one day. I was so happy with what I learned about myself and women, I cried.

Your book is making a difference already. I recently met a . . . caring, sensitive, loving, active and physically beautiful woman. . . . I go past her house to go to work. I stopped for a paper. I saw her favorite gum, bought a pack, wrote a note and left it in the doorway. One thing led to another. A few weeks after our first night "MAKING LOVE," (it was the most fabulous night I ever had, except for the ones since then), I wrote her a "FAIRY TALE." It was a fun story about how we met and the events leading to our first night together. . . . I cannot believe the fun I'm having and I cannot believe the women who have asked me out. I've had to turn them all down because I now have a lover who is dominating my every thought. . . . I'm not afraid of anyone stealing her away from me. . . . I'm armed and dangerous. I carry a copy of *Light Her*

Fire. . . . Thank you, thank you, thank you for helping me become a "REAL MAN."

Here's a letter from Louis:

I recently purchased a copy [of *Light Her Fire*] and have read it twice and learn more each time I read it. . . . I am thirty-three years old and was divorced almost three years ago. In reading the stories of men who took your class it was almost like I was the one telling the stories. . . . Ellen, if your book would have been four years earlier chances are that I would still be married!

However, I am thankful that I am not. I recently went out on a date with a woman I work with, and the mutual sparks could have set a city block on fire. I have never felt so strongly about someone and the possibilities for a long-term relationship as I do about this one. The greatest thing about this is that now I know what to do, thanks to your book. I will not let this one slip through my hands.

You're never too old to learn something new, as this letter from a sixty-nine-year-old (young?) man proves:

. . . I'm the kind of a person that always has a book with me in case I have to be away from home waiting for something. This time I had a pizza to wait for before taking it home but nothing to read. At the supermarket next door I spied your book. I have always been curious about what women tell other women about men. But more than that, I thought, perhaps I can learn something from your book.

... It doesn't take much of an idiot to turn things around and recognize oneself front and back. For example, I'm a neatnik and my wife is the other way, but after twenty years of marriage I'm STILL trying to change her. Oh, I've lightened up a great deal (she hits back!) but the urge is still there. Now, BY GOD, with your help, I think I'm going to be able to knock off that crap once and for all.

One of my favorites is from Dick:

I just wanted to pass on my personal experience to add to your collection of testimonials. When I was returning from a recent trip in NYC, I picked up *Light Her Fire* in [the airport]. As I read it on my way [home], I chuckled and said to myself, "You have a Ph.D. in Mathematics and a preschool education in love." (I have been married to my only wife of 31 years.) ... I thought that I would give your ideas a try. ... I got her a ... card in the airport. ... I also included a note which said I brought her three presents: *The first to tell her how I feel about her, the second to say how sweet she is, and the third to say how loving she was.* The first was a small bag of peanuts I saved from the flight. I covered up the "pea" to say that I was "nuts" about her. The second was a delicious chocolate cookie I saved from the flight to say how "sweet she was." The third was a box of Good and Plenty (these are a favorite of hers and an idea of yours) to say that loving her was "good and plenty."

(Total investment in these presents was $3.05 and the payoff was equal to a fur coat.) I left the room after giving her the card and presents. When I returned she was wiping a couple of tears away (she almost never cries). I then sat down to ask her how she was doing, how her job was going, etc. She talked on and on as I listened and asked more questions. Then she asked me if I wanted a drink (that's a sign that love making is next). I said sure. Later I showered, jumped into bed, and found her just as you predicted.

What fun! I'll always carry *Light Her Fire* with me in my briefcase to use as a resource to remind me how physical I am and how psychological she is. It's really that simple. Thanks.

The following letter made me cry and has stayed in my thoughts for over a year:

. . . I wandered into the bookstore. . . . One book was sticking out from all the others and I looked at it and saw it was your new book, the one I was hoping you would write. Without even opening it I took it up to the counter and paid for it. . . . Later that same day we piled up in bed to read. . . . I had replaced the cover on *Light Her Fire* with a cover from a nature book called *Quiet Magic*. She would have been upset if I was reading a book called *Light Her Fire*. . . . The next day I followed some of the advice and for the next couple of weeks I kept it up and you know what? I can't explain it but I've fallen in love with my wife all over again. Maybe you should have called this one *Light His Fire* because it feels like I lit my own fire and it burns in me. A man must fan his own fire before he can light another one. And now for the "pièce de résistance." Last week my wife went in for a breast biopsy. Her mammogram had shown something. We are anxiously waiting for the results. I am so fortunate to have fallen in love again with her before all this talk of breast cancer. Knowing I did all those loving and romantic things before the mammogram has a very special meaning to both of us. And whatever the results, I'll always be alongside her. I want to thank you from deep in my heart for the love and joy that was uncovered in me. Your book is a godsend. Why it was sticking out all by itself I'll always wonder. What kind of coincidence was it that the cover of the book I used to hide your book was *Quiet Magic*? I'll never understand, but all that has happened sure must be a little piece of life's magic which I wanted to share with you.

LITTLE THINGS MEAN A LOT (TO A WOMAN)

Megan wrote to let me know how her life has changed:

I am writing to thank you for making me so happy. My boyfriend, Les, bought your book *Light Her Fire* about a month ago and since then my life has been total bliss! I can't believe how much he has changed in so little time. Before the book, he never held my hand when we were walking together and never came over to me if we were at a party. Now, he *always* holds my hand and even compliments me in front of his friends! Yesterday, I wasn't feeling well and he sent me some beautiful flowers. To most women that might not seem like much, but to me it really meant a lot. He is so considerate now that sometimes I wonder if I'll ever be able to reward him enough for making me so happy! I cannot tell you how many examples of "the wrong way to act" were true for us, but now everything has changed. After reading the book, Les actually told me he couldn't believe I stayed with him for six years because of the way he used to treat me. I stayed because I really loved him and I hoped that someday he would change. Well that day has come, and I can tell you that I love Les more than ever. Thank you so much for writing a book so that men can finally understand women!

A woman who signed her letter as "Your Fan" writes:

I mentioned to my husband that I had a book I wanted him to look at. I knew he was busy and probably might not want to read the entire book, so I . . . highlighted . . . the twenty or so pages that I thought were the highlights of the book. He agreed and hasn't been the same since. He opens the car door, holds my hand everywhere, loads the dishwasher without me asking, asks if he can prepare dinner, or if he can get me anything! I'm in heaven!

Marianne has a wonderful way of expressing what she's given and received as a result of reading *Light His Fire*:

I just finished your book today. . . . I can't tell you how good I feel and how much closer my husband and I have become. I actually caught myself daydreaming this afternoon after reading the section about "Make A Wish." I thought how nice it would be to get flowers from my husband again—like I used to. I love fresh flowers and I used to tell him so.

Well, just a few minutes ago the owner of one of our local florist shops delivered two dozen of the most beautiful long-stemmed red roses I have ever seen. I was so thrilled I started to cry—I thought the florist was going to cry too, as he explained that my husband wanted me to know how much he loved me and how special I was.

My husband left on his annual motorcycle trip to Mexico with the "guys" this morning but he found time to think of me. I sure am glad I put the little card in his backpack which says:

> Have a great time but remember . . .
> You won't find a señorita as sweet
> A Margarita as intoxicating
> Or a tamale as hot
> AS I AM!!!! Hurry Home—I Love You.

This letter makes me laugh every time I picture the scene Gloria so humorously describes:

Since Valentine's Day was approaching and I am allergic to chocolate, my dear sweet husband (of 36 years) always gets me something I want very badly. So this year I asked for . . . *Light His Fire*! Valentine's Day I went up to the attic, got our son's gun and holster set, his cowboy hat and my white cowboy boots. I undressed and got the three cowboy things on. It was dark. I turned all the lights off, except the light on the stairs behind me. He opened the front door, there I stood in the foyer (one foot on the top basement step). I drew the toy pistol and said, "Drop your pants!" His mouth flew open (the door still open too), my present (your book) *had* been under his arm—now on slate floor, mouth still open and so was door! The barrel of the pistol came uncocked and fell downward, but my husband became cocked and flew upwards! I'm sure you have the picture! What a way to receive your wonderful book! . . . We plan to ride the range together for the rest of our lives.

Finally, this letter shows just how creative you can be, even with a tight budget:

. . . I saw you when you appeared on "Sally" and even though our budget is very tight (we have six children) I went out and bought your book.

. . . I'm a housewife and we live in [the Midwest], so about this time of year I get the midwinter blahs extremely bad! Especially being cooped up in the house with six children, plus the five I baby-sit for. I played out one of my favorite fantasies. I planned a beach party! It consisted of a bottle of wine, *submarine* sandwiches and two new tapes which neither of us had heard before. One of the tapes had ocean sounds. . . . I also went out to buy my husband a new pair of swim trunks (something skimpy) but this time of year I couldn't find anything so I improvised and bought him some BVD bikini briefs. I wrapped them with a little poem that said, "Put these on. We've our very own beach in our bedroom on top of the sheets." It was the nicest thing we've done in a long time. It cost about the same as a night out without the expense of a baby-sitter. Our two older children thought it was pretty great that mom and dad were having their own little party in their room that no one else was invited to. All the kids were in bed and were tucked in for the night and I could really enjoy getting to know my husband again without worrying about the kids. (I usually do if we go out.) We actually enjoyed our food too. With six kids at the supper table it's hard to eat anything, let alone enjoy it. Anyway thank you again.

CONTENTS

Six

DECORATING WITH LOVE IN MIND

Seven

NOT TONIGHT, DEAR, THERE'S A CHILD IN OUR BED!

Ten
EVERYONE DESERVES TO FEEL GOOD

Conclusion

INTRODUCTION

A NEW BOOK IS BORN

While promoting my books on a national tour, I was a guest on a radio program that invited listeners to call in with their questions or comments. I had just finished giving a lengthy list of romantic tips that were guaranteed to *light a fire*, when a woman called and said I obviously didn't have children. When I explained that I had three, she was shocked. Then, in an almost desperate plea for help, she asked, "How can we light a fire when the kids are driving us crazy?" Since there is so little time on TV or radio to give a complete answer to a complex problem, all I was able to tell her was that the best gift you can ever give your children is a loving relationship with your mate. I remember wanting to give her so much more information and thinking, To answer that question is a whole other book.

Well, here it is.

This book is for every couple who wants to recapture that sexy, sensual time when you and your mate delighted in each other, paid devoted attention to each other, and were turned on by each other. Thousands of couples like you have learned that they don't have to settle for a boring, humdrum existence just because they've become parents.

No matter how ready they think they are, few couples are ever really prepared for the changes that take place when a child enters their life. We can get vocational training to learn how to fix a car; we can get an advanced degree in teaching; and we can learn to paint at art school. Unfortunately, there are no schools to teach us about life. The only training you get in being married and raising children is OJT (on-the-job training).

If you were fortunate enough to have been raised in a home by two parents who were romantically in love with each other, had great communication skills, and were devoted parents with a lot of common sense, you probably have a few more partnership and parenting skills than most of us. If your parents had an unexciting marriage, were only together for the sake of the children, or were terrible parents, your skills need to be upgraded.

You deserve a better, more exciting relationship than your parents had. You want to do better and stop the pattern that has been handed down from generation to generation, but you don't know how. By declaring that you want more out of life than your parents had; by realizing that you have a choice; and by taking a good look at what you learned from them and deciding whether it is valuable or destructive, you can follow a different path.

My classes have included parents who have never been married, parents who have been married two or more times, and parents who were married to their one and only spouse. Because of the many different family structures existing in the world today, in this book I have used the broader terms "mate," "partner," and "relationship," rather than the more restrictive terms "husband," "wife," "spouse," and "marriage," to denote the romantic relationship between a couple who are raising children together. Rest assured that the principles in this book apply whether you are a natural parent, stepparent, adoptive parent, foster parent, or any combination of the above—married or single.

After fifteen years of teaching about relationships, raising three children to adulthood, and having a thirty-year love affair with my husband, I believe I've earned the right to share my thoughts and ideas with you. My personal and professional experience enables me to tell you emphatically that you can awaken all those wonderful romantic feelings that may have been dormant since your children were born. I promise you that if you will apply the principles taught in this book and do the homework assignments at the end of each chapter, you will have a romance with your mate that most people only dream about, and you'll become a better parent as well. Being a parent can be one of life's greatest joys, if you understand how to deal with the challenges a new life brings to the relationship.

Learn how you can have a love affair with your mate while raising your children. Join me as I teach you how to fall in love with your mate all over again. Join me as I take you on a different path—one where happiness, love, romance, excitement, communication, and passion await you.

DO YOU NEED THIS BOOK?

If you're not sure whether you can benefit from reading this book, take this quiz and find out.

1. If my mate were to make a list of priorities, I would be:
   a) At the top of the list
   b) Near the top of the list
   c) Somewhere in the middle
   d) At the bottom
2. If I told my mate what I need to make me happy, my mate would:
   a) Do everything in his or her power to grant my request
   b) Make a reasonable effort to grant my request
   c) Make a halfhearted attempt to grant my request
   d) Ignore my request completely
3. When was the last time you gave each other a passionate kiss?
   a) Last night
   b) Last week
   c) Last month
   d) I can't remember
4. When was the last time you made love?
   a) Within the last few days
   b) Within the last few weeks
   c) Within the last few months
   d) When our last child was conceived
5. When is the last time the two of you went out on a romantic date alone?

    a) Last week
    b) Last month
    c) Last year
    d) Before we got married

6. When is the last time you went on a vacation alone together?
    a) Six months ago
    b) One year ago
    c) Five years ago
    d) On our honeymoon

7. When is the last time you made love somewhere other than your bedroom?
    a) Within the last week
    b) Within the last month
    c) Within the last year
    d) I think sex should be in bed, under the covers, with the lights out.

8. Sex is:
    a) A pleasure that I enjoy
    b) A way of satisfying my partner's needs
    c) A way to get what I want
    d) An obligation

Give yourself: 4 points for every A answer
              3 points for every B answer
              2 points for every C answer
              1 point for every D answer

Results:

32   A perfect score. You have a wonderful relationship, and you are still lovers. You're probably the envy of all your friends. You could have written this book yourself.

24–31 You have a good relationship, but there is definitely room for improvement. This book will enhance what you already have.

16–23 Your relationship needs your immediate attention. Find a quiet place, read this book cover to cover, and do your homework assignments as soon as possible.

8–15 Your relationship has nowhere to go except up. Keep this book as a constant companion. Don't lend it to anyone!

One

✳

AN OVAL-SHAPED SOUL
ON A ROUND PLANET

THE PROPER-SHAPED SOUL

Years ago, I read a story about a young girl who was fed up with her parents for trying to force her to be like everyone else. This girl had a theory that since we live on the planet Earth, and it is round, we assume that all the other planets must also be round. Her premise was that God saw many different-shaped planets: some round, some square, some oval, and so on. She explained that when you are born, God is in charge of matching your soul to the proper-shaped planet. If you had a triangular soul, God would put you on a triangular planet. If you had a square soul, you'd be sent to a square planet, and if you had a rectangular soul, you'd live on a rectangular planet. This young girl felt that, in her case, God had really goofed! She had an oval soul, and He had put her on a round planet. Everyone was trying to change her oval soul to a round soul so she could fit on this planet, when all she ever wanted was to keep her oval soul.

This story causes me to wonder how many parents try to change the souls of their mates, as well as their children, into the "proper"-shaped soul—whatever that is. Too often, it's having a child who believes what we believe, behaves the way we behave, and wants what we want.

After I discussed this subject in one of my lectures, a woman approached me at the break and confided that she had taken her daughter, who just couldn't conform to the family's values, to a number of different psychologists over a period of years. Finally, one of the doctors took the woman and her husband aside and told them, "What you want to do is take a forty-year-old brain and put it into a sixteen-year-old girl. Well, it can't be done!"

Every family must have room for different-shaped souls. Every human being is unique, yet for many parents the challenge of child rearing becomes to try to mold their child into what they consider to be a perfect person. This struggle to change a child's soul so that he or she mimics our likes, dislikes, personality, spirit, and dreams inevitably results in total frustration on our part as we drive our child crazy.

YOU'VE CREATED LIFE. NOW LET THEM HAVE IT!

As far back as 1923, Kahlil Gibran, poet and philosopher, gave this advice to parents in his book *The Prophet:*

> You may give them your love, but not your
>   thoughts
> For they have their own thoughts.

I remember one very wise woman who decided that it was not too late to change her mind about an important decision she had made some time ago. Her eldest child, her son, had been in college for six years, had hated every minute of it, and wanted only to be out in the work force. "He's not lazy," Eleanor said. "He's always had a job and knows exactly what he wants to do. Perhaps his career choice—a racetrack announcer—would not be mine, but he's good at it and loves it. However, I've been pushing him to finish school, for my sake and his father's."

After the class discussion, Eleanor called her son in Lexington, Kentucky, and told him that she loved him and wanted him to be happy. "Perhaps someday he'll finish college—when it suits him," she said, "but now he needs to follow his own star and not mine. I cannot tell you what a tremendous burden has been lifted from my shoulders. It feels so good to finally let my son live his own life in his own way."

I know for some of you it would be easier to read about how to change your children than it is to read about changing yourself. It's always easier to blame others for driving us crazy, even our children, than it is to blame ourselves and change our own actions and attitudes. No one ever said life was easy.

WHY YOU DO WHAT YOU DO

Even though we have the best of intentions as parents, we often place unnecessary pressure on our children and in the process drive ourselves crazy.

Many parents view their children as an extension of themselves. These parents push their child to live their unfulfilled dream, become what they didn't become, accomplish what they didn't accomplish, or finish what they never finished.

Tim, a large, well-built man, told the class that as an adolescent he had been very tall and skinny, and as a result he was shy and withdrawn. He longed to play football, but because of his build he could only fantasize about what it would be like to be on the team and be sought after by the prettiest girls in the school. When Tim's son graduated from eighth grade, Tim sent him to football camp so he could be trained, to enhance his chances of winning a place on the high school football team. When the son returned from camp with pain in his lower back, X rays determined that his spine did not line up correctly with his tailbone. The doctor felt that any hard blow to the back might cause permanent injury. His advice was to find another sport. Tim confessed that "when the doctor gave the diagnosis to my son, it felt like he was giving it to me. *We* were never going to play football. All the old feelings of isolation, failure, and inadequacy that I felt in high school came rushing back to me.

"Absorbed in my own misery, I didn't answer my son when he turned to me and asked, 'Are you mad at me, Dad? I've disappointed you, haven't I?'

"On the way home," Tim continued, "my son astonished me with his well-balanced attitude. He said not getting to play football really wasn't so bad. He had already decided that, since he liked politics and debate, if he couldn't participate in sports, he'd become active in the student council and run for office."

His son's response made Tim realize that his son had just been trying to please him all along. After much soul-searching, Tim decided that he couldn't live vicariously through his son anymore. He had to

Finally, many parents view their relationship with their children as their primary relationship and their relationship with their spouse as a secondary relationship. They rely on their children to give them the pleasure and gratification that they should be getting from their marriage. These parents will put their children first and their own needs last. They have made a heavy investment in the parent-child relationship, and they expect a good return on their investment. They expect too much from their children. All of their energy goes toward watching, guiding, evaluating, and judging their child's behavior. This constant preoccupation with their children is often a way to avoid the real issue—lack of attention and affection between the parents.

Children do not need this kind of care, nor do they benefit from always being the center of attention. They usually get a rude awakening when they grow up and realize that the world doesn't revolve around them.

Most of all, they can never repay the debt such a parent *thinks he is owed.*

While discussing this topic in class one night, Margaret, a woman in her late thirties, volunteered that this message really hit home with her. She had spent the last three years totally immersed in her daughter's cheerleading activities. She attended all of her workouts and competitions. During football season, she spent every Friday night at the high school football games, and during basketball season she never missed a basketball game—just to cheer her daughter on. Prior to Margaret's taking my class, she noticed that her daughter began to resent her involvement. Margaret confessed that her daughter's lack of appreciation hurt her feelings. As Margaret began concentrating on her marriage, she began to do some soul-searching.

"What I realized," she said, "was that my constant involvement in my daughter's life was due to a void in my own. Now I know that my daughter didn't need a constant chaperon or companion. She had plenty of friends. I'm the one who needed to be involved. Now that my husband and I are spending more time together, I find that my daughter is actually relieved. She told me she was always worried that I had nothing to do, and she felt responsible for my happiness. What a burden for a sixteen-year-old."

Dan, a graduate of "Light Her Fire," told the men one night that he had spent every evening with his fourteen-year-old son helping him with his homework whether he wanted help or not. Dan had been an excellent student himself and felt his guidance would help his son excel in high school. "When it finally dawned on me," he said, "that I was spending more time with my son than with my wife, I realized that I was putting my son's interests ahead of my wife's needs. The reason I'm in this class is because my marriage was falling apart. Now that I'm really focused on making it work, I find that my son can do just fine without me. If he needs my help, he just asks for it!"

As the students in my classes learned to focus on their relationship with their mates, they gradually became able to admit that their children had their own lives to live and needed freedom from parental scrutiny in order to shape their own lives. My students no longer needed their children to bring them the joys and fulfillment that had been missing in the relationship with their mates.

BECAUSE YOU ARE MINE

There is a big difference between encouraging a child to develop *his* talents and follow *his* dreams and pressuring him to follow yours. Every human being is unique and should be loved and appreciated for who he is, not what you want him to be.

You have to send a message to your children that no matter what they do or don't do, it has nothing to do with your love for them. I have used a book in my classroom for years called *The Way Mothers Are* by Miriam Schlein. It's the story of a little kitten who asks his mother why she loves him. When she asks him to guess, he thinks of the times he's good and says she must love him then, but she certainly can't love him when he's not behaving and not doing what he should. At the end of the story, the mother says, "You don't think I love you just when you're good, and stop loving you when you're naughty, do you? That's not the way mothers are. I love you all the time, because you're mine."

I love you because you are mine! This is the message we all need to hear—especially our children—over and over again from our families.

We've become a nation of people who are always interested in doing, accomplishing, and producing instead of *being*. As families, we must let other family members know they are valuable human beings simply because they exist! We should send the message to one another that no matter what we do or don't do, our value as human beings remains the same. Our children, as well as our mates, need to be able to say, "I may have failed this test, but I am not a failure."

I recall an evening a few years ago when my daughter's girlfriend Suzie was having dinner at our house, and the girls were discussing their progress reports. Suzie commented, "Boy, if I ever brought home a C on my report card, my parents would die!" It concerned me that Suzie was so worried about her parents' reaction to a C. I felt compelled to caution her. "Suzie," I said, "at some time in your life, you may possibly get that C. Life is not made up of all A's and B's."

When I discussed this with my class, one of the students, who happened to be a psychologist at a major university in the area, spoke up. He stated that he was seeing suicidal freshmen and sophomores who had gotten straight A's all through high school. Now, for the first time, these straight-A students were receiving B's, and in some cases, C's and D's. "It's so tragic," he said with despair in his voice. "They want to end their life over a grade."

I'll never forget Bonnie, a woman in her early forties who told one of my classes that she was a perfect example that what I was saying was true. Her own daughter had tried to commit suicide. Bonnie explained that although the family had rarely spoken of failure, it was understood that it could not be tolerated in any form. Both she and her husband were very high achievers. They had Ph.D.'s after their names, and they expected their children to follow in their footsteps. While their son was an outstanding student, their daughter had always found school to be a struggle. When their daughter realized that she had failed her math class and it was only a matter of time before the dreaded report card came home, she tried to kill herself rather than deal with her parents' disappointment. Bonnie wept as she said, "Thank God we got a second chance to let her know how much we love her. That math class, or all of her classes, for that matter, were totally insignificant to us. What mattered was our daughter."

Bonnie went on to say that after this incident she spent a great deal of time finding out what her daughter wanted to do with her life. They switched her from honors classes to regular classes and supported her decision to go to a junior college until she decided what she wanted to do next.

YOU'RE ALWAYS BEING TESTED

When your child asks a "what if" question, such as "What happens if I don't pass that test?" you are being tested as a parent. A typical parental reaction to such a question might be "What do you mean, if you don't pass? If you study, you'll pass." What your child really wants to hear is "Nothing will happen. You'll still be my child, and I'll always love you. You can only do your best, and if you fail, nothing is going to happen. You'll come home, I'll give you a kiss, and we'll review the exam and see what you missed, so that you'll understand it better next time."

When my oldest daughter graduated from high school and decided to attend a college three thousand miles away, she agonized the entire summer about her decision. "What if it's the wrong choice? What if I'm making a mistake?" she asked over and over. My reply was always the same: "Nothing will happen. You'll come home and make a new decision." With this kind of reassurance, a child feels comfort. Compare this with a similar situation involving friends of ours. When their son decided on a particular college, he asked the same question. His parents replied, "What do you mean, what if it's wrong? You made your choice, and you'll have to live with it!" They went on to tell him how expensive it was going to be to send him to college, adding that if they were going to spend that much money, he'd better stick it out.

Do you see how differently these two teenagers will feel, leaving home for the first time? Both will go with uncertainty, but at least my daughter has the comfort of knowing hers is not a one-way ticket, while our friends' son has the stress of feeling it's "do or die."

Earlier I talked about how parents try to change the souls of their children into the "proper"-shaped soul. Not surprisingly, many marriages fail because we try to change our mate's souls. People who ask, "Why can't my mate understand that my way is the right way?" are involved in a no-win power struggle, when they should be respecting, and even enjoying, souls of a slightly different shape.

HELP! WE DON'T AGREE ON ANYTHING— ESPECIALLY HOW TO RAISE OUR CHILDREN

In my books, *Light His Fire* and *Light Her Fire,* I explained how opposites attract. Your differences attracted you to each other at the start of your relationship. Most people are attracted to someone who possesses traits they lack themselves. His strengths are your weaknesses, and your strengths are his weaknesses, like two pieces of a puzzle that fit together. You are completely different human beings. That is why each parent has a unique way of relating to his or her child. We are all different—not better or worse, not good or bad, not right or wrong—just different.

One of the most frequent arguments between parents involves how to raise the children properly. I maintain that there is no one proper way to raise a child.

When I started teaching evening classes, I had to organize my time and my household duties to make life easier for myself and my family. Part of the agreement with my family was that, on the nights that I taught, I would prepare dinner in advance and leave it for them to heat and serve. In return, my husband and children would clean up, because I was too tired to do it when I came home from teaching. One morning when the children came down for breakfast, they said they were starving. When I asked them, "Why are you so hungry? Didn't you have dinner last night?" they replied, "No. We told Daddy we didn't like what you made, so he told us not to eat it, and he cleared the table. So, instead of eating, we played awhile, and then went to sleep."

I couldn't believe my ears. How could he just let the poor kids go hungry? When I asked him why he had done that (actually, it wasn't exactly a question—it was more of an accusation), he answered, "Because they said they didn't want the food, and they weren't hungry. Did you think I was going to beg and plead with them like you do?"

The amazing thing is that they never rejected another meal while he was in charge.

One night in class, a group of women compared the differences between how they relate to their children and how their husbands do. Patty, a woman in her thirties, laughed as she told us, "When I take my four children to a fast-food restaurant, it takes at least fifteen minutes for everyone to agree on where to go. Usually, it's a screaming match, and we wind up going with whatever three of the four agree on. But when my husband takes them out, he decides where they are going, and if he hears them complain, he'll turn the car around and go home. Guess what? With him, they never complain. Of course, you can tell who the 'softie' is in our family, and who is more of a disciplinarian.''

We all agreed that Patty wasn't wrong and her husband right or vice versa. They were just two different people who must respect each other's way of relating to their children. With Patty, the children get a chance to voice their opinions, disagree, get angry, and vent their feelings. With their father, they learn rules, time management, and the art of compromise. And children are geniuses at knowing what works with one parent and what works with the other.

TWO AGAINST ONE

Although conventional wisdom dictates that it is very important for both parents to be in complete agreement about a particular situation, behavior, or request that involves their child, I've always felt it was ridiculous to try to fool children by presenting a united front about our feelings.

If we think about what determines our individual feelings and reactions to any situation, we realize it is a combination of:

• How we were brought up
• Our basic personality

- Our personal experiences
- Our intuition and insight

Since no two people on earth have the same up-bringing, personality, experiences, and intuition, everyone is unique. It is not only unrealistic, but terribly unfair, to expect one parent to behave according to the other's values, needs, or expectations. In any given situation, one parent's feelings and reactions might be completely different from those of his or her mate, so that one parent must cover up his or her genuine feelings in order to present a "united front."

Children can actually see what's going on anyway. They know exactly which parent is lying and pretending to agree with the other, a situation that can leave the child feeling angry and resentful toward the deceitful parent.

My student Carolyn admitted she was upset when her husband, Bill, failed to support her when she had a confrontation with their thirteen-year-old daughter about her messy room. In reality, Bill couldn't care less about his daughter's room. He had enough trouble himself abiding by Carolyn's rules to pick up his own belongings. Eventually, Carolyn came to realize that if Bill went along with her expectations and pretended to care about a neat, clean, organized room, he would be discounting his own feelings. In fact, she was relieved to learn that she could set limits and insist on a certain behavior from her daughter without making Bill pretend that he felt the same way.

The next week, Carolyn returned to class and told everyone how she used her newfound knowledge. This is how she explained things to her daughter: "Look, Shannon," she said, "your Dad doesn't really care one way or the other about your room, but I ca very much because of my upbringing. You know, when I was a child, we were very poor, and I was always ashamed of my house. I never wanted to bring friends home to that 'pigsty' we lived in. I promised myself that when I had a home of my own, it would be neat and clean so that I would never be ashamed again. We are very lucky to have a beautiful home, but I need your help so that I don't carry the burden of cleaning this whole house by myself." Together, Carolyn and her daughter made a list of chores that Shannon would be responsible for, and Carolyn told the class that her daughter had done every chore on the list all week.

The point I'm trying to make is that you need to get comfortable with the fact that in many areas of being a parent, *you stand alone*, and that's okay. You are entitled to feel what you feel, be who you are, react the way you react, and, in short, be real.

John, whose five-year-old son loved to play with his trucks, army soldiers, and miniature hot rods, told the class one night that his wife couldn't stand the noise that resulted from the sound effects that went along with destroying the enemy, beating the competition, or crashing the cars and trucks. John said, "Her nerves are shot. She's gone back to school to get a degree, and she has a lot of studying to do. She expects a five-year-old to keep quiet. Well, I love the fact that he can keep himself amused for hours. When she tells me to 'shut him up,' I feel like a phony when I tell him to settle down and stop making that noise. The truth is, I like his noise. I love the sounds he makes."

John really understood my point that he could be true to his own feelings while still respecting his wife's needs. He decided to approach the problem in a different way. He went home that week, sat his son down, and told him they needed to have a serious man-to-man talk. He told his son that Mom becomes annoyed and upset more easily these days because she has a lot of pressure to pass her tests. He also told him that they'd both try to help while she was studying. "If I'm not home," he said, "you try to do some quiet-time activities, like coloring or playing with your sticker collection, or watch TV, or listen to your story tapes. When I get home, I'll take you to the park, and you can scream, yell, run, jump, and make all the noise you want." He said his son gave him his promise that he would be quieter with Mom when she had to study in return for a noisy time in the park.

Instead of John feeling like a phony for pretending to agree with his wife's feelings, it's important for him to be as honest with his son as he can be about what's really going on. A child can accept an honest, clear message that goes along with a parent's true feelings.

OPPOSITES HAVE DIFFERENT PARENTAL VIEWS

Of the thousands of parents who have been through my seminars, those who have raised happy, healthy, productive children concur that the best role models are parents who respect their own and each other's differences. The child automatically learns to value both points of view. Because you are opposites and tend to balance each other out, you are actually going to raise a very well balanced child. Very often:

- A father's love is liberating
- A mother's love is suffocating

- A mother makes a child feel lovable
- A father makes a child feel competent

The following are areas of potential conflict for parents:

- One parent feels the child should be picked up immediately when he or she cries.
- The other parent feels the child will be spoiled if he is picked up and should be left to cry.

- One parent feels it's important for a child to discover things on his own through trial and error.
- The other parent feels that a child needs to be closely guided so he doesn't make mistakes.

- One parent feels a child should be in bed by 7:00 P.M. in order to get the proper rest.
- The other parent feels the child should stay up as late as she wants and fall asleep when she is tired.

- One parent feels that it's important to include the child in every outing.
- The other parent feels a competent baby-sitter should watch the child, and the parents should go out alone.

- One parent feels that it's important for the child to play a competitive sport.
- The other parent feels that learning to cooperate is much more important than competition.

- One parent feels it's important to establish routines and schedules.
- The other parent feels children have an innate sense

of what's best for them and should be allowed to establish their own schedule.

You probably have some conflicts of your own that you could add to the list.

THE ART OF COMPROMISE

There is no one perfect solution to a conflict. There are usually many options to be discussed. The art of compromise can be made fairly simple as long as you don't have the attitude that your mate is wrong and you are right. It's important to understand what it is in your partner's past that makes a particular issue important. Then, from true understanding, you can come up with a solution with which you both can live.

To help you compromise in the face of a dilemma, ask yourself:

"Keeping in mind that my mate is the most important person in my life, how can I solve this conflict and still validate my mate's feelings without discounting my own?"

For example, Joan's husband came from a very strict upbringing. As a child, he always had to be in bed by 8:00 P.M. He vowed that if he ever had children, there would be no set bedtime, and they would establish their own sleep patterns. Joan, on the other hand, felt a loss of intimacy in their relationship because she never got to be alone with her husband. She wanted to cuddle in her husband's arms and have some adult conversation, but their eight-year-old required constant attention. Finally, after both had attended my course, they sat down and decided to compromise. The outcome was that Gina, their daughter, was allowed to stay up as late as she wanted on weekends, but on weeknights she would go to bed at 9:00 P.M. and get a good night's rest. That would give Joan two hours of uninterrupted time with her husband, since she never went to bed before 11:00 P.M.

The art of compromise will be discussed in more detail in Chapter 9: "It's What You Say *and* How You Say It."

BECOMING ASSIGNMENTS

This book is meant to help women and men as they struggle with their roles as individuals, partners, and parents. It is designed to help you resolve the daily conflicts of meeting each other's needs while meeting the children's needs and finally coming to terms with it all. Unless all these areas are addressed, peace and harmony in your life as a couple will always elude you.

My seminars were so effective because they were never just theory or rhetoric. At the end of every session, there were homework assignments—things I wanted the students to say or do. Since this book is based on the seminars, I want you to pretend you are taking a course rather than just reading a book. Instead of lending your copy of the book to a friend, have her get her own copy, because what's meaningful to you may not apply to her. Underline things you need to remember or use a yellow highlighter so that this book becomes a guide you can refer to over and over again. You will also need to invest in two different colors of index cards on which you can make notes to yourself about the homework assignments.

One color will be devoted to becoming a better *parent*, the other will be geared toward becoming a better *partner*. Keep these cards with you at all times, so that you will have constant reminders at your fingertips.

I once met an elderly gentleman from India who told me that he never thinks of himself as a human *being* because *being* implies stagnation. He liked to think of himself as a human *becoming*, which implies growth. My homework assignments will be geared toward growth in two areas:

1. Becoming a Better Parent
2. Becoming a Better Partner

The first homework assignment—"Becoming a Better Parent"—is designed to help you help your children feel better about themselves and feel more secure knowing how much you love them. As I taught my seminars on how to "Light His Fire" and "Light Her Fire," many of the men and women applied the principles I taught, not only to their mates, but to their children as well. Some of the parents were separated or divorced. Others were happily married, but the children were beginning to cause havoc in their lives. All the parents in my classes agreed that when the children were happy and secure, it was much easier to concentrate on the romantic side of their life together and put more energy into their relationship.

Together, we discovered that the same principles that work for a forty-year-old man or woman also work with a four-year-old child or a fourteen-year-old teen. As many of my students began to apply the principles I taught, not only to their relationships with their mates but to their relationships with their children, they would come to class and share the amazing results they had experienced. Little by little, their success stories became part of my teaching, and what started out as a course on men and women relating to each other evolved into a course that included ways to relate to your children as well as your mate.

The second homework assignment—"Becoming a Better Partner"—is designed to bring you and your mate closer together. Your focus here is on each other. This is the opportunity to strengthen and deepen your relationship and commitment to each other. By doing these assignments, you give your mate the ultimate gift—the gift of your time and your love.

ASSIGNMENT #1

Becoming a Better Parent

As a parent, the best gift you can give your children is a belief in themselves and their worth.

This week, give each of your children a big hug and kiss and say, "Have I told you lately how glad I am that you are my daughter (or son)? You have added so much to my life. I wouldn't trade you for any other child in the entire world. I really love you for who you are. I can't imagine what my life would be like if you weren't a part of it."

Stand back and watch your child beam.

By the way, I don't care if your child is three or thirty-three. I want you to say this no matter what age your child is. If your children don't live with you anymore, pick up the phone or write a letter. Just tell them what a blessing they are.

Becoming a Better Partner

Not only do we have to appreciate our unique children, we also have to appreciate our unique mates. The best gift I can give my husband is to let him know that he is a wonderful father and a terrific husband. It makes him want to be even better.

It's music to my ears when he tells me how much he admires me as a wife and mother. I love it when he takes me in his arms and tells me how lucky our kids are to have me as their mother. All women need to be validated in their roles as mothers by the men in their lives.

Whether you are reading this book alone or together, give your partner a big hug and kiss and tell him or her how much he or she matters in your life. Turn to him or her and say, "I want you to know that I love you and appreciate you with all my heart. I never thought I'd feel so fulfilled and happy. You've made my life so complete. I wouldn't trade you for any other man (or woman) on this earth. I love you with all my heart. You are the best father (or mother) a child could ever hope for and the best lover that anyone could ever dream about."

Two

✳

HE'S X-RATED, SHE'S PG

THE TWO SIDES OF SENSUALITY

When Myrna and Phillip signed up for my class, they looked very familiar. It turned out that I had seen them at various school functions, as both their daughters attended the same high school as mine did. One night Myrna came to class early, and we began to talk. I remember being very excited about a movie my husband and I had seen the previous evening. I asked Myrna if she had seen it yet. I'll never forget the scornful look in her eyes as she replied, "My husband and I *never* [she really emphasized the word "never"] go to an R-rated movie. We *only* see PG-rated movies." For a moment, I felt very uncomfortable. I wanted to say, "Well, pardon me," but I let it pass.

A few months later, my husband and I were returning some videos we had rented at a neighborhood video store. As we stood in line to pay, who should emerge from the back room where all the X-rated movies are located but Phillip. In his arms, he carried a stack of adult movies. I can't describe the discomfort we both felt when our eyes met. His face turned beet red, and with a quivering lip he said, "Myrna has gone to visit some relatives for a week, so I thought, Oh, what the heck!"

I smiled politely and said nothing. As we drove home from the video store, I told my husband about my classroom conversation with Myrna some months back. My husband and I both felt sorry for a forty-year-old man who felt he had to sneak behind his wife's back to enjoy adult movies.

When I write the word "sensuality" on the blackboard in my men's class and ask the men to tell me what the word means to them, most describe sexually explicit encounters with one or more naked women making love to them. In other words, they pictured X-rated sex scenes.

When I ask the women in my class the same question, the responses include such romantic encounters as a man and woman dancing close together, lovers holding hands while walking on a moonlit beach, or a man and a woman gazing lovingly into each other's eyes over a candlelight dinner. In other words, a woman's idea of sensuality is definitely rated PG.

Obviously, men and women are different. A man gets excited looking at pictures of women in alluring outfits, negligees, erotic poses, and so on. Sometimes just a woman with long legs or large breasts will be enough to arouse him. A woman, however, gets more excited by words. She loves reading romance novels, while he enjoys *Playboy*. After observing men and women for more than a decade, I can honestly say that most women truly don't understand how strong a man's sex drive really is. Men, on the other hand, do not have a clue how emotionally starved most women are.

So the question is, how can someone who is X-rated live happily with someone who is rated PG? The answer is for each to be able to understand the other's basic needs and to do everything in his or her power to fulfill them. It is my firm conviction that the biggest difference between a man and a woman is that:

A man needs sexual fulfillment in order to respond to a woman emotionally.

A woman needs emotional fulfillment in order to respond to a man sexually.

Rather than waste time trying to prove you're right and she's wrong . . . or you're good and he's bad, why not decide that you'd rather be loved than right. When you each learn to fulfill one another's needs, you can have a satisfying sex life that is good for each of you, both physically and emotionally.

Over the years, I've asked the men and women in my classes to tell me what it was about their mate or their relationship that made them feel loved and content. It's interesting to note that most of the answers given by men seem to refer to their physical needs being met, while most of the answers given by women seem to refer to their emotional needs being met.

Men Said, I Know She Loves Me Because:

- She calls me at work and leaves an erotic message on my private line. There's no need for me to ever call those "love" lines.
- She's great in bed. She enjoys sex as much as I do.

As Paul Newman says, "Why go out and get hamburger when you've got steak at home?"

- She's always coming up with new places and ways to make love. I never know what to expect.
- She's always a pleasure to come home to. She has a smile on her face, and she stops whatever she's doing to greet me.
- She tells me often what a great lover I am and how much I satisfy her.
- She's very affectionate. Not a day goes by that she doesn't kiss me and touch me.
- No matter how busy she is with the kids, she always plans for us to spend time alone together.
- She's the most capable person I know, and yet she always makes me feel needed.
- She makes me feel like I'm the sexiest man alive.
- She's very playful and always knows how to get me to laugh.
- I've never been jealous in all our years together. She only has eyes for me.
- She's got great hands. She gives me the best massage.
- I travel a lot, and she always makes my homecoming special. I feel like a VIP.
- She has no sexual hang-ups. She does to me what other men only dream about.
- I can tell her anything, and she'll always be on my side.
- She thinks I have a great body even though I'm a bit out of shape.
- She's always interested in what I do, think, and feel.
- She always discusses things with me before making an important decision, even though she doesn't have to.

Women Said, I Know He Loves Me Because:

- He never complains when I serve him leftovers. In fact, he tells me they taste even better on the second day.
- Whenever I point out a beautiful woman or a woman with a great figure, he tells me he doesn't think she's anything special. Then he tells me why he thinks I'm prettier and sexier.
- He'll take our children shopping with him, just so I can have some time to myself.
- He usually calls me a couple of times a day just to see how I am and to tell me he's thinking of me.
- He always remembers my birthday, our anniversary, Valentine's Day, and Mother's Day with a gift.
- He brings me flowers just to let me know how special I am.
- I have to be careful what I ask for, because he always gets it for me.
- Whenever I call him at the office, he's always available. Even though he's very busy, he never hurries me, and he never cuts me off because of another call coming in.
- He tells me he loves me every single day.
- He's very supportive and caring. He's always there for me to lean on.
- Whenever I go somewhere that is unfamiliar to me, he maps out the directions. He always wants me to call him when I arrive, so he knows I'm safe and sound.
- He never goes to sleep without kissing me good night, and he always wakes me with a good-morning kiss.
- When he gets up in the morning, I'm usually sound

asleep, but he never leaves without giving me a kiss. Even though I'm asleep, I feel his kiss, and it stays with me all day.

- He buys sexy underwear in different colors and prints. He says he wants to look good for me inside and out.
- Whenever I ask him to do me a favor, whether it's getting me a glass of water or going to the store, he does it with a smile on his lips and love in his heart.
- If he's going to be late getting home, he always calls me.

Many years ago, "Dear Abby" printed a letter she received from a fifty-year-old woman who said that after thirty years of marriage, she wanted to forget about sex completely. She said she felt she had paid her dues. Like most women (she said), she got very little physical satisfaction from sex and she was just going through the motions for the man she loves. She signed her name "Tired." Abby asked her readers to reply. Of the 250,000 women who responded, more than half agreed with "Tired."

When I read this, I felt sorry for "Tired" and all the other women who were "just going through the motions," and my heart went out to every man who lives with a woman like this.

IN DEFENSE OF MEN

Imagine what it must be like to live with a woman who is paying her dues or fulfilling an obligation. A man wants to feel loved, not endured. A woman who *sacrifices* her body for her partner's sake is not doing anyone a favor, including herself. A man whose mate simply tolerates sex feels diminished, both sexually and emotionally, and is likely to seek a sexually satisfying relationship elsewhere. We've all heard stories about successful politicians, actors, ministers, and other highly visible men who risk everything they've worked so hard to achieve for the sake of an extramarital affair. It doesn't matter who he is or how successful he is, every man wants to feel wanted and needed physically.

A woman who enjoys sex and is an active partner doubles the pleasure a man derives from sex. The men in my classes have told me that they really want their mate to be responsive:

"Although it's great to have a woman be concerned about my pleasure and satisfaction," said Taylor, "I want the same for her. The ultimate turn-on for me is when she's turned on. I love knowing she wants me sexually."

Larry agreed. He said, "I want my wife to be as interested in sex as I am. That's why I'll do anything, including prepare dinner and clean up the kitchen, so that she has a chance to relax and get in the mood after the kids go to sleep."

Men love to hear that you enjoy what you do together sexually. A woman who sees sex as her duty will never give a man the emotional satisfaction of feeling desirable, and will, in turn, never get the emotional fulfillment she needs. Some women worry that a man will think less of them if they pursue him sexually, but most men find it refreshing if the woman is the aggressor occasionally. As Al put it, "Sometimes it's great to be able to just lie there and be passive. I think it's every man's fantasy to be treated like a sex object once in a while."

IN DEFENSE OF WOMEN

If a woman is not getting her emotional needs met, it is almost impossible for her to respond sexually. For a woman, kindness, gentleness, devotion, commitment, caring, attention, patience, and compliments are sexy. For a woman, the desire for sex results from feeling cared for, cherished, and loved. It starts early in the morning when her mate kisses her and says, "I love you." It continues during the day when her mate phones to say, "I was just thinking of you." Stopping at the supermarket, doing your fair share of the chores, being an involved father, and noticing how pretty she looks all make a woman more open to sex. A woman whose mate takes the time to let her know that she's special, needed, appreciated, and loved will be far more available sexually than a woman who is neglected or ignored. "Tired" and the more than one hundred thousand women who agreed with her cannot be getting their emotional needs met. If they were, they would definitely feel energized and excited about sex. In the course of my career, I've talked to enough women to know that those "tired" women who hate sex are the same women who wind up having an affair with the man who gives them the affection, attention, and conversation they've been craving for years.

TRADING SEXUAL ROLES

Many times over the years, I've had both partners in a relationship taking my classes at the same time—

one in my men's class and the other in my women's. They both complain that they are unhappy with how often they make love. Usually, the woman complains it's too often, and the man complains that it's not often enough.

I've found a wonderful way for a couple to arrive at a happy medium in the frequency of their love-making. I have the woman in the relationship take on the sexual role of the man for two weeks, and I have the man take on the sexual role of the woman for two weeks. She can be as aggressive as she wants, and he can be as passive as he wants. The challenge is for the woman to try to think like the man, and vice versa. It may sound impossible suddenly to become the opposite of what you've always been, but pretending makes it possible. You tell yourself it's okay to be a certain way, because it's not *really* you. You're just acting. "It's not really me," "It's just an assignment," or "I have to do it for the sake of my relationship"— it doesn't matter what you tell yourself to make the switch. You'll be amazed at how completely you are able to get into your role, once you've given yourself permission. Your actions, thoughts, and feelings will really become characteristic of the role you are playing, because the mind cannot differentiate between what's real and what's make-believe. Your mind reacts to whatever you tell it. What happens is similar to what occurs when two actors are given a script and told to *act as if* they are madly in love with each other. Often, they wind up having a passionate affair off-screen as well as on, and what starts out as pretense becomes real. The power of suggestion is so strong that, even in the presence of the entire film crew, the two people involved become so convinced by their performance that a real romance develops.

Here's what Joe said after he and his wife, Alice, completed this assignment.

"I used to think that sex was purely an animal instinct. You didn't need to prepare anybody for sex, you just did it! It annoyed me that my wife couldn't get in the mood unless we first spent time with each other. She wanted to cuddle, talk, have me brush her hair, massage her neck, all of which I considered a waste of time. When we reversed roles, I was surprised at how much I enjoyed asking for a massage, soaking in the tub, or taking a shower together, and generally playing hard to get. The more I wanted to set the scene for making love, the more she just wanted to do it! I really think this assignment taught us to understand that we could both have our needs met."

The long-term effect of this exercise is that a couple seldom revert completely back to their old ways. They come to realize the importance of satisfying their partner's needs in order to get what they want. The woman tends to become bolder and more aggressive, and the man becomes more romantic. Role-playing or role reversal sure beats the alternative of drifting apart and resenting each other. The technique has helped many couples get through some rough times. For example, Mel reversed roles with his wife, Lorraine, at a time when she needed it most, even though Lorraine had to give Mel a rain check for her role at a later date. "My wife was really sick during her whole pregnancy. Medications didn't help her constant nausea. I guess you know what that did to our sex life. But every time I began to feel sorry for myself, I tried to put myself in Lorraine's shoes. There's no way for a man to really know what it's like to be pregnant, but by looking at it from her point of view,

I found myself trying to make her life as easy as possible. The wonderful thing about giving is that you do receive. Now that our baby has arrived, I'm cashing in my rain check, and we're making up for lost time."

For the woman, pretending to be a man can be a very liberating experience. Shirley said, "The first time I tried this, I realized how exhilarating it was to put all thoughts aside and just enjoy the physical act of sex like my husband usually does."

Alyssa liked being the one to decide when and where on the spur of the moment. "I've always enjoyed making love, but it takes a lot of time and planning with three kids around. It's kind of fun to just think *sex*. The spontaneity is a turn-on, and best of all, it takes no planning. I used to think my husband was wrong to want sex without any preparation or planning and I was right to want to set the stage for romantic lovemaking. Now I realize that the combination of romantic lovemaking once in a while and having spontaneous sex other times is the best of both worlds."

If we don't put a value judgment on our differences, we really can learn from each other. To be a truly a great lover, a man must be sensitive, understanding, compassionate, patient, and kind. This doesn't happen overnight. It takes years of being with a woman who is a great teacher. By the same token, with the right man, a woman can learn to relax and enjoy sex. If the man she is with is open and comfortable about sex, a woman can learn to appreciate her own body and completely let go, offering her mate not only her body but her movements, sounds, and unrestrained responsiveness.

THE TWO-WEEK RULE

Many men and women feel confused and frustrated when they try to figure out what it is that will please their mate, while others seem to know instinctively how to make their partner happy. You don't have to be a mind reader to know how to please your lover. In most cases, it's not even necessary to ask them what they want. All you have to do is stop, look, and listen. Closely observe what your mate does for you, wait two weeks, and then do the same thing for your mate. Sound simple? It is, but often it's the simplest things that bring about the most happiness and change. Here's how this works:

- She calls you at work just to let you know she's thinking of you. Wait two weeks and call her with the same type of "I was just thinking of you" call.
- You're right in the middle of preparing dinner, and he starts to "fool around." Wait two weeks, and when he's busy doing something, begin "fooling around" with him.
- She writes you a love note and leaves it in your lunch box or briefcase. Wait two weeks, and leave her a love note on the refrigerator or bathroom mirror.
- She entertains the kids all day on Sunday, while you enjoy a football game with your buddies. Wait two weeks, and give her the day off while you take care of the kids.
- She massages your neck and shoulders while you are reading the newspaper or watching television.

Wait two weeks, and while she's watching television or reading a book, give her a relaxing massage.

Hugs, kisses, conversation, surprise gifts, and anything else your mate does for you are a clear indication of what your mate really wants and needs. If every couple were to practice this exercise faithfully, the divorce rate would drop dramatically, because everyone would be getting his needs met. By paying close attention, you'll see how much your mate craves what it is that he or she is giving or doing for you. A man who feels at a disadvantage because he isn't imaginative, creative, or romantic is probably with a very creative, romantic, imaginative woman, since opposites attract. All he has to do is watch what she does, wait two weeks, and do what she did. He'll hit the mark every time, because he'll be acting on the clues she's given him. This exercise also solves the problem for women who complain that they aren't sexy enough. Watch his gestures and just do to him what he does to you. Oh, how I love simplicity!

AND BABY MAKES THREE

If you and your mate are about to become parents for the first time, you are probably experiencing a wide range of feelings—mostly positive. No doubt, you are also experiencing some negative feelings. Having a baby is a very big step, and a permanent one. After all, it's not as if you can return Junior to the department store if you change your mind!

Starting with the first few weeks of pregnancy, the changes a baby makes in your life are profound. First will be the physical changes experienced by the mother-to-be as her body nurtures the growing life within it. Along with that will be emotional changes as the expectant parents adjust to the knowledge that their lives are about to be changed forever. New stresses will be placed on the relationship, as the new mother- and father-to-be attempt to redefine their roles. Unfortunately, many women become so focused on the changes taking place in their bodies that they become insensitive to their husbands' needs.

One night in class, Ted, a young lawyer in his late twenties, talked about the changes that had occurred between him and his wife since she became pregnant.

"When we first found out that Donna was pregnant, we celebrated for a week. We had been trying to have a baby for three years and were thrilled when the news we had been praying for became a reality. We were so close those first few months, as we shared in the anticipation of our first child.

"I think I first noticed the change taking place in our relationship during Donna's fourth month of pregnancy. That's when she began to feel the baby move. At first it was so exciting to put my hand on her stomach and feel the baby kicking. However, I'll admit that the novelty began to wear off for me as Donna kept grabbing my hand every ten minutes. I noticed a distinct decrease in Donna's involvement with me as her involvement with the baby growing inside her increased. Donna's a teacher, and before she became pregnant, we always enjoyed telling each other about our day. Then everything began to change. Donna bought every book ever published on pregnancy, babies, and parenting. Every evening she'd sit down with a book and find fascinating tid-bits that she just had to underline and remember.

Slowly, I felt she was entering a private world that I was not part of.

"Whenever I did tell her about something that I thought was interesting, she'd interrupt me right in the middle of a sentence with, 'Hey. The baby's kicking again,' or 'I wonder if that was a hand or a foot that time?' There was no way I could compete with 'motherhood.'

"Now the baby is a year old, and our marriage is headed for divorce court unless we can pull it back together somehow," he lamented.

Though he was ashamed to admit it, Ted, like so many men, began to feel increasing resentment toward his unborn child. Meanwhile, Donna, like so many women, became so involved with motherhood she never even noticed Ted's feelings of isolation and loneliness. Donna became less interested in sex, while Ted's sexual desire increased because of the lack of intimacy he was feeling. Ted wanted the same kind of love and closeness that had existed between them before this intruder came into their lives. Before, Donna had been his wife and lover. Now, she was clearly a mother with a capital *M*.

So begins the distancing between a couple who once couldn't keep their hands off each other. The thought of an affair had crossed Ted's mind, but he had never acted on it. Fortunately, although frustrated, he had remained faithful, so it was relatively easy for me to put this relationship back together and bring back all the "lovin'" feelings they had once shared.

I've seen so much pain caused when a man is unfaithful while his wife is pregnant or just after the birth of their baby. Stan was one of those men. He took my class in an attempt to win back his wife, Terri.

"My life is falling apart," he divulged. "After the birth of our son over a year ago, my wife had no interest in sex. She ignored all my advances and always had an excuse as to why sex was impossible. I couldn't believe this was the same woman who used to come to my office with nothing on under her coat. She had such a wild imagination! Now all of her attention was focused on our son. I became so lonely that I got involved with someone in my office. I did it out of desperation, and I know it was wrong. When my wife found out, she took the baby and went to live with her parents. I really love her and miss her. Please help me get her back," he pleaded.

At my suggestion, Terri enrolled in my class, and eventually she did return to Stan. She told the class, "Before my pregnancy, I was very satisfied with my appearance, and I was used to getting appreciative looks from men. Then, I gained a lot of weight, more than I should have, and I kept a lot of it after the baby came. I felt fat and ugly, and all of a sudden I realized that no one, including my husband, was looking at me in the same way as they used to. I know Stan wanted sex, but I didn't feel sexy, and he sure didn't let me know that he felt I was attractive or sexy."

Stan and Terri began to date again and share their feelings. Terri's sexual desire returned, and Stan was grateful that he didn't lose his wife, knowing that his infidelity could have caused the separation from his wife and child to be permanent rather than temporary.

PLEASE DON'T TOUCH

For many women, the physical changes that occur during pregnancy interfere with their sexuality. Jeanine recalls that during her first trimester she was so sick that she couldn't smell any food without becoming nauseated. As she said, it's hard to think about sex while you are throwing up! Patricia said she remembers being so tired she could hardly keep her eyes open, and Nancy was distraught about the extra weight she gained. "It was hard to feel sexy carrying around an extra sixty pounds," she cried.

This is a time when a woman really needs comfort and reassurance from her mate. Fluctuation in sexual desire happens to all people at different times in their life, for either biological or psychological reasons. It's normal and is usually a temporary situation. Eventually, a woman's sexual desire will return, but it can take some time. What she needs more than anything from her mate is unpressured cuddling, holding, touching, and kissing, and most of all, to know that he still finds her sexy.

Even after the baby is born and the doctor says she can resume sex safely, a woman may not be feeling sexual. Her breasts might be tender, whether she's breast-feeding or not. She may have acquired stretch marks that she finds embarrassing. Add to that an expanded waist, larger hips, and extra weight, and you have a woman who's desperately depending on her mate to reinforce her sexuality.

CONFIDENCE IS SEXY

Although men and women may have different ideas about sensuality, the one thing both seem to agree on is that self-confidence is sexy. According to the women in my classes, self-confidence is sexier than any particular physical attribute.

Christy says, "A sexy man is one who is comfortable with his body and isn't awkward and shy."

Maria says, "A sexy man is one who thinks he's sexy. He walks, talks, and thinks with a sexuality that is very attractive."

Likewise, the majority of men I've asked feel that a truly sexy woman is one who feels good about her body, regardless of its size or condition. According to one man, a sexy woman is one who radiates confidence and is comfortable about her body. Another one said, "It's a woman who feels sexy with her clothes on or off."

It's too bad we don't live in the time when the full-figured woman was the ideal. Today's media have us brainwashed into believing everyone must have a thin, hard body, even though that's not the norm. Accept your body with all its flaws and allow yourself to feel sexy. Your body is the one that your mate wants to make love to. Every wrinkle, line, and stretch mark represent the new life you created, the precious time you've been together, and the memories you'll have forever.

JEALOUS OF YOUR OWN CHILD

Even though a man can never have the biological experience of pregnancy or childbirth and cannot possibly understand the psychological turmoil that accompanies so many physical changes, he has his own adjustments to make. His wife's breasts, which he once enjoyed caressing, are now reserved for the child. He and his wife are both responsible for a new life, and the demands on both of them are great. Many men have said that they are jealous when they perceive the new baby as a threat to their relationship. Calvin said he didn't like having to share his wife's love with their son. He wanted to be the center of her universe, and Terence said, "Watching my newborn nurse, there's no doubt in my mind how much my wife and my daughter need each other. But where do I fit in?"

A mother may also feel hostility toward her child if she finds her husband paying more attention to the child than he does to her. Dixie admitted this was her problem. "Kevin used to call to tell me he loved me. Now he only calls to see how Amber, our two-year-old daughter, is doing. As soon as he comes home, it's Amber who rushes into his arms. Then it's an evening of watching Kevin and Amber talk, sing, and play. I know I should be thankful that he's such a great father, but I'm jealous and want my husband back."

This is a time when both partners need to feel loved and desired. Each waits for the other to give a kiss, a hug, a massage, anything to show he or she cares. Neither does anything. Both are disappointed and angry. Each thinks, It was never like this before we had a kid!

The most important thing to do during this crucial time is to be sensitive to each other's needs and to share your feelings. Don't be afraid to admit that you feel jealous, resentful, or hurt. I have found that many couples are ashamed of their feelings, thinking it's not right or "normal" to feel what they feel. Fear that your feelings are unacceptable will cause you to hide them and will interfere with open communication. Such a lack of communication can eventually destroy a relationship.

ASSIGNMENT #2

Becoming a Better Parent

Children who are raised in a loving environment where sex is discussed openly grow up to be self-confident, sexually responsive adults.

1. Teach your child to love and appreciate his or her body. Just as you name other parts of the body correctly, do the same with the genitals. Making up nonsensical names such as "pee pee," "wiener," or "do-hickey" gives children the message that there is something wrong with their sexual organs and makes them uncomfortable about their sexuality.

2. Be prepared to talk about sex openly with your child and to answer his questions as they occur. Your child should have the benefit of learning about sex in a warm, open, loving discussion from a parent who cares. If you are uncomfortable about your ability to do this, the following books can help

you explain a subject you may find difficult to discuss:

- *Where Do Babies Come From?* by Margaret Sheffield (for ages five and up)
- *What Is a Girl? What Is a Boy?* by Stephanie Waxman (for ages three to six)
- *Talking with Your Child About Sex* by Mary S. Calderone, M.D., and James W. Ramey, Ed.D. (anticipates questions asked by children at different age levels)
- *Where Did I Come From?* by Peter Mayle (ages six to ten)

Becoming a Better Partner

1. Plan to make love to your mate within twenty-four hours of reading this chapter. If you are a woman, prepare yourself mentally to be sexual. If you are a man, prepare your wife for lovemaking by being loving and attentive.
2. Reverse roles for two weeks. If you are usually the seducer, become the seducee. If you are usually the seducee, become the seducer.
3. Together, discuss how your lives have changed since the children came along. Share your fears and inner feelings. If there's been a great deal of distancing, promise to rectify the problem, making each other's needs your main focus from now on.
4. Begin the two-week rule. Observe your mate and make note of what he or she does for you. Wait two weeks and do the same for him or her.

Three

BRING BACK THAT
LOVIN' FEELIN'

FROM MOMMY AND DADDY TO LOVERS

One of my favorite stories is about a couple who are having a problem making love. They go to a sex therapist, who asks them what they think the problem is. They are very uncomfortable and fidgety, and finally, the man turns to his wife and says, "You tell him, Mother."

A good place to begin your transition from Mommy and Daddy back to lovers is to take a look at how you refer to each other. Think back to the pet names you called each other before you became parents. Honey, sweetheart, darling, lover boy, or stud muffin are just a few examples of some loving ways to call out to your mate.

Pet names are a very loving and intimate way of speaking to your lover. In my book *Light His Fire*, I had a long list of pet names. Believe me, *Mother* and *Father* and *Mommy* and *Daddy* were not part of this list! If you and your mate are in the habit of using this kind of maternal or paternal label when you refer or speak to each other, stop doing it now!

Grown men do not think of their mothers as sex symbols, and grown women don't want their daddy for romance. If you call each other Daddy and Mommy too often, that's how you begin to see each other. Once we see ourselves or our mate as simply a mom or a dad, rather than as a lover, it is difficult to have passionate sex.

Carrie complained that when her husband comes home from work he often has that "poor me, I had a terrible day" look. She knows he wants sympathy and a neck rub, but she's been mothering three kids all day, and she really doesn't want a fourth. "Just once," says Carrie, "I want him to burst into the house, grab me in his arms, and give me a passionate kiss. All of this poor-baby stuff is fine, but later, when he wants to make love, I feel like his mother, not his lover."

William has lost his sexual urge for his wife, Phyllis. He says when he gets home from work, she greets him the way a drill sergeant would. "Instead of a welcome-home kiss," William said, "It's 'Don't forget to wipe your feet,' 'Hang up your jacket,' 'Be ready for dinner in ten minutes,' 'The mail is on your desk.' I feel like I'm at home with my mother. All I do is fantasize about other women."

I remember one time I was a guest on a radio talk show and the subject of pet names came up. The host told me and his many listeners that after fifteen years of marriage and three children, his wife still lovingly uses a pet name she gave him before they were married. He told us, "Whenever she writes me a note, she addresses it to CB. When she calls the station to leave a message for me, she refers to me as CB." Since I was dying of curiosity, and I knew the listeners were, too, I had to ask what CB stood for. "It stands for cannon balls," replied our host. I was speechless and didn't have any kind of a comeback, so I quickly went on to another topic. We both giggled through the rest of the show. I was pleased that he had been willing to reveal the playful way his wife refers to him in private. Of course, it wasn't private anymore! He was truly a lucky man to have a woman who remained his lover after all those years.

THE GREETING

Another area that can usually stand improvement after children enter your life is the way you greet each other after being separated for the day. Think back to the time when you first fell in love. How did you greet your lover after being apart for the entire day? You couldn't wait to see each other, right? That's because you each knew, without a doubt, that you were the most important person in the other's life. Both of you felt special, important, needed, and desirable. Every time you saw each other again after being apart . . .

- You stopped what you were doing
- You smiled
- You embraced
- You kissed

Compare that greeting to today's. How do you greet the most important person in your life now?

- Are you busy on the phone?
- Are you working in the yard?
- Are you talking to a neighbor?

- Are you working in the kitchen?
- Are you involved with the children?
- Are you working on the computer?

If so, how do you think your mate feels? Your husband or wife probably feels as if he or she is at the bottom of your list of priorities. When other duties, like opening the mail, attending to chores, or taking care of the children become more important than greeting our mates, we've lost a very important part of our intimate relationship. It's sad but true that most people spend more time greeting their pets than they do their partners.

In *Light His Fire*, I gave a lot of attention to my homework assignment "The Ten-Second Kiss." I instructed couples that whenever they hadn't seen each other for a long period of time, they were to wrap their arms around each other and give each other a kiss that would last a minimum of ten seconds. I don't care if it lasts longer than ten seconds, but it can't be less. Obviously, I'm not talking about a brother-sister type kiss. I'm talking about a long, passionate kiss.

After the book came out, I received many letters from readers who now practice the Ten-Second Kiss every day.

Becky writes, "No more pecks on the cheek for me. I now kiss George with my mouth and entire body every morning before we leave for work. Thanks to the Ten-Second Kiss, we start out each day excited about the coming evening when we can be together again."

Another woman writes, "After reading your book, I changed my end-of-the-day routine completely. I took your advice, and now, instead of making sure dinner is ready, I make sure I'm ready for Tom's homecoming. The first time we really kissed, he nearly went into a state of shock. He shook his head in disbelief as he said, 'Boy, what's gotten into you? Are you sure you are still my wife and the mother of my kids, or did someone else step into your body?'

Always remind yourself how you would greet your mate if you were having an affair with him or her. If you engage in a long, intimate kiss as you part for the day, you'll have a mate who can't wait to step through the front door in the evening. And if you greet each other with the Ten-Second Kiss when you see each other again at the end of the day, you'll see that your whole evening will feel different. You can still go about your routine activities, but you'll feel so much more connected.

Kids who run to the front door to greet Mommy and Daddy have to be taught that they are second in line. First Mommy and Daddy are going to kiss. Then it's the children's turn. Make it your goal to get to your mate before the kids do. Cathy, a graduate of "Light His Fire," related a cute story about her Ten-Second Kiss. When she decided to incorporate the Ten-Second Kiss into her nightly greeting to her husband, she explained to her two children, ages eight and eleven, "From now on, when Dad comes home, he and Mommy are going to kiss for at least ten seconds." That evening, when Cathy's husband came home, her youngest son ran to the microwave and set the timer. He said he wanted to make sure they really kissed for ten seconds.

A LOVER'S PROGRAM

Whenever my students complain to me that their mates are preoccupied with the children and their sex lives have become nothing more than fantasy, I always ask them the following questions. Answer these questions yourself to see how healthy your marriage is.

- When was the last time the two of you went out alone on a date without the children, without friends, without business associates, and without other family members?
- When was the last time the two of you went away alone for an overnight stay or a weekend at a hotel without the children, without friends, without business associates, and without other family members?
- When was the last time just the two of you went on a trip or vacation without the children, without friends, without business associates, and without other family members?

If your answer to any of these questions was something like "I don't remember, it's been so long ago," or "It's been a few years," or "Not since we had our first child and she's eight now," your marriage is in trouble!

THE ONLY WAY TO FLY

One night, as I was discussing the need for parents to take vacations without the children, a student named Steve spoke up.

"I'm so glad to hear you say that," he said. "Years ago, my wife and I tried to take our kids with us on our week's vacation, and it never worked for us. We couldn't afford to pay for airfare for five of us, so we got into the car instead. What a disaster. Not only did the kids fight most of the time because they were too cramped and bored in the backseat, my wife and I fought all the time, too.

"I always started out with a plan and a destination for the day. Usually, it was farther than my wife thought was reasonable. Of course, we were always behind schedule because I never figured on the number of stops we'd have to make. It seemed as if somebody *always* had to go to the bathroom. We'd just get on the road again after a potty stop, when someone else would have to go. After a full day of stopping and starting, stopping and starting, listening to the kids fight over who had whose crayons, or like one time finding the crayons melted in the back window of the car, Natalie and I were not in a very romantic mood. We always arrived at the motel much later than we expected, and we always took longer to get started in the morning. It's kind of funny looking back at it, but it sure wasn't funny at the time. By the end of the 'vacation,' we were hardly speaking to each other, and the kids didn't have fun, either.

"Your class confirms what we had come to believe ourselves—that we needed to go on a vacation for just the two of us to renew our closeness as a couple. In a way, the way things worked out was probably a blessing in disguise. The kids have never resented us going alone, either. In fact, as they got older, they enjoyed their time alone and were happy to see us go.

"We look at our vacation as a couple and the family vacation very differently now. If it's to be a family vacation, then it is geared to the kids, and we know there will be no opportunity for us to be alone. This way, we have no expectation that we will be able to act as lovers, and no one is disappointed. We always have a great time, now."

Couples whose marriages not only survive but thrive long after the children leave home have one thing in common. They always take the time to be alone together. Without privacy, there can be no romance. Somehow, happy couples know instinctively that by making each other their number-one priority and meeting each other's needs, their children will grow up happy and secure.

What unhappy couples do not understand is that if they make their children their number-one priority, thinking they can work on their marriage later, they'll probably wind up as one of the *one out of every two* marriages that end in divorce today. Not only will your children grow up and leave you, but your mate will grow away and leave you, and you'll wind up all alone. Many couples mistakenly believe that the only thing lack of privacy prevents is sex, and they rationalize that they can do that after the kids go to bed. Being alone, having quality time with your mate, is much more than sex. It's necessary to have time alone to focus on your partner. It's imperative to have time alone to give each other that which is so desperately needed in a relationship—your undivided attention.

Dual-career families have unique demands on them. Often, one or both partners must travel separately for business, so that time at home is at a premium, and finding time to be alone together is a tremendous challenge. Yet when the job demands it, there always seems to be time available for business-related social events. Your time together as a couple must be treated as a priority that is every bit as important as the time you spend with clients or business associates, and should be scheduled accordingly.

The program I'm about to discuss is absolutely,

positively necessary if you want to remain lovers while raising your children. This is not to be regarded as something that sounds nice and you might try sometime. It's a program you must follow if you want your relationship to be successful. None of the successful professionals I know leave their career to luck or chance. If I told you I had the perfect formula for achieving wealth and success in your professional life, would you follow it? Of course you would! Well, I do have the perfect formula for success in your love life, and I'm going to share it with you now.

HAVE AN AFFAIR

What follows is the formula for having an affair with your mate that will last a lifetime.

- Make one night a week date night. It doesn't matter which night you choose. Just pick a night you can both agree on and stick to it. The only requirement for how you spend this evening is that you spend it alone together. No children, no friends, no business associates, no other family members for the entire evening. Your focus is to be on each other.
- At least once every three months, have a weekend away, or at the very least, an overnight stay at a hotel with an early check-in and a late checkout. No children, no friends, no business associates, no other family members for the entire weekend. Most couples have a honeymoon after their wedding—a time to focus on each other as husband and wife away from family, friends, and pressures. Think of your quarterly weekend getaway as a minimoon. As I said, at least four of these are needed each year to

renew your love and commitment to each other.

• Once a year, plan a one-week (that's seven days) vacation—for just the two of you. No children, no friends, no business associates, no other family members. Most people can manage to take two weeks off during the year. You can use the second week for a family vacation, or to stay home and catch up on projects. You must have one whole week's vacation together every year if you want your relationship to thrive. If you stop to think about it, you'll realize there's no way that the two of you would have gotten married in the first place if you hadn't spent time alone as a couple. Well, a good rule of thumb to remember is that *whatever you did to win your mate, you need to do three times as much to keep him or her.*

If you doubt the importance of sticking to this program, consider the following:

• If you don't have an affair with your mate, you risk the possibility that someone else will.
• The best gift you can ever give your children is a loving relationship with each other.
• The happiest, best-adjusted children come from a home in which the parents love each other.

THE OBSTACLE COURSE

Very few things in life that are worthwhile are easy to achieve, and a loving, lasting relationship is no exception. Of course there are obstacles to be overcome in your quest for a terrific marriage, but together we'll overcome each obstacle, one at a time.

OBSTACLE #1—YOU CAN'T FIND A BABY-SITTER

Yes, you can, but it might take a while before you find someone with whom you are comfortable. In my own case, I wanted a mature woman when my children were infants. Later, when the children were very active, I felt more comfortable with a teenager, someone young enough to get down on the floor and play with them. I spent a great deal of time and energy getting referrals, interviewing, and calling references before making a choice I felt good about. I knew, as I'm sure you do, that finding the right baby-sitter was worth any amount of time and effort. When you are sure that you have found the best-qualified person with whom to entrust your children, you can relax in the knowledge that they will be well taken care of, and you won't be phoning home every hour to check on things or worrying every minute that you're gone.

You might find, as I did, that it works best to hire someone to baby-sit on a regular basis. Since you've made a commitment to make one night a week date night, hiring a regular baby-sitter will work to everyone's advantage. The baby-sitter will set aside that night for you, so that you won't have to spend time each week searching for a sitter. Since the sitter is counting on the job, you'll be less inclined to back out of your commitment to each other. Having the same sitter each week has the added advantage that your children will become well acquainted with the sitter instead of having to adapt to a new person each time.

My own daughters baby-sat regularly for two of our neighbors. One particular couple used my oldest daughter every Saturday night, and another couple used my younger daughter every Friday night. The girls looked on their baby-sitting as a regular job, so they were always available. Whenever they got a call from another family wanting them to sit on a night they had reserved, they had to decline because they already had a commitment. It's important to have one or more sitters as backup, so you are not frantically looking for an alternative in the event your regular sitter is sick or has an important event to attend. In the case of my daughters, if something important came up for one of the girls, her sister could always fill in for her.

There are several ways you can go about finding a baby-sitter who fits your needs. You can:

- Call baby-sitting agencies.
- Ask friends and neighbors for their recommendations.
- Call the local high school and ask the guidance counselor for a list of responsible students.
- Ask your pediatrician for referrals.
- Call a local elementary school or nursery school. Many times a teacher or teacher's aide is willing to baby-sit for an evening or a weekend. If your schools are closed during the summer, teachers may also be available to sit while you take your week's vacation.
- Check with your church or synagogue. Sunday school teachers, students from the teen group, the young parents' group, or even the seniors' club, if there is one, can offer assistance with baby-sitting.
- If finances are a big problem, check with the parents of other young children in your neighborhood or social group to see if they would be willing to exchange baby-sitting with you on a regular basis.

- You can call a nursing registry in your area if you want someone who knows CPR or is well equipped for emergencies.
- Don't forget the grandparents. Even if they both still work full time, they may be thrilled to be with their grandchildren for an evening, a weekend, or a week. Just be sure they have the option to say no if they have other plans or feel it would be too much for them. And be sure to let them know how much you appreciate them when they do baby-sit.
- You can advertise in your local paper for precisely the type of baby-sitter you want.

Once you have acquired a list of potential sitters, it's time to start the interview process. When you first call the potential sitter, you can ask some preliminary questions to find out how well he or she fits your criteria. For example, if sitters need to provide their own transportation, you can find out over the phone whether or not transportation is available to them. If they don't have their own transportation and you are willing to pick them up and drive them home, then they need to be geographically close to you, so ask them in what general vicinity they live. Whenever I hired a teenager, I liked her or him to live close by, and I always liked to meet the parents. It made me feel more secure to know there were caring parents nearby in case of an emergency.

If the sitter seems like someone you might be interested in hiring, invite him or her to come over and meet your children. This way you can see how they interact firsthand.

During the face-to-face interview, it's a good idea to tell the baby-sitter exactly what you expect of him or her. This way you can get a sense of how he or she reacts to your rules. If you don't want her or him on the phone because you'll be checking on the kids and you want the line clear, say that in the interview. If you don't allow sitters to have their friends over, be sure that's clearly understood. If they seem uncomfortable with the idea of limiting their phone calls or not having visitors at your house, you'll want to look further.

Ask each potential sitter about his or her previous experience, and obtain a list of references. Make sure you call all the people on the list. Find out how long the reference has known the sitter and how the reference feels about him or her. If she or he no longer sits for the reference, find out why. Encourage the reference to speak freely by asking open-ended questions—i.e., tell me what you liked about so-and-so; what didn't you like; how did your children react to him (or her); and so on.

You can use open-ended questions when interviewing potential sitters as well. Another good way to find out more about the sitter than surface things is to set up a scenario—a hypothetical situation—and ask the sitter what he or she would do. If you have an infant, you might ask, "What would you do if my child wouldn't stop crying?" If you have a toddler, you might ask, "What would you do if my child started choking on a toy?" Their answers don't necessarily have to be the one an experienced professional would give, but they should reflect thoughtfulness and a basic awareness of what constitutes an emergency.

The first time you have your new baby-sitter watch the children, it's best to plan to stay fairly close to home and to limit your time away to a couple of hours. Of course, you will have prepared your children ahead of time for the fact that you have found someone very special to take care of them while Mommy and Daddy have their date. Even if you think they are too young to understand, you can talk to them about your plans. It'll help you make the important transition from being there with them to leaving them in the care of a trusted sitter, and it will establish a pattern for you to follow on future date nights.

Allow plenty of time to acquaint your sitter with the house, the children, the pets, and your rules before you leave. Use the following checklist each and every time you leave the children with a sitter, to ensure that all these important items have been discussed and are thoroughly understood.

Checklist

1. Prepare and display prominently a list of:
   The telephone number and address where you can be reached. If it's a movie theater, get the direct line, not the information line.
   - The telephone number of your pediatrician
   - The telephone number and address of the nearest hospital
   - The telephone number of the local police department, fire department, and ambulance service. If you have 911 service, be sure the sitter knows to use it in an emergency.
   - The telephone numbers of two or three responsible adults who are close by and available in case of an emergency
2. Give the sitter a tour of your house. Show him or her the location of the telephones, flashlights, candles and matches, fire extinguisher, and first-aid supplies.

3. Show the sitter where the circuit breaker is and explain how to reset it in the event of a blown circuit.

Prepare a list of rules of the house and be sure the
sitter understands them. If your children are old
enough, go over the rules out loud so that the child
hears them, too. Some of the issues you may want to
address are:

- Is the sitter expected to feed your child? If so, what?
- Is the sitter expected to bathe your child?
- Can your children watch TV? If so, what?
- What time your children are to go to bed
- Your child's normal bedtime routine, i.e., tooth
  brushing, potty stop, braiding hair, and so on
- If your child wears diapers, show the sitter where
  they are and which ones your child wears at night
- Is the sitter allowed to help himself or herself to
  snacks, and if so, what?
- Are your children allowed to eat in any room of the
  house, or are they restricted to the kitchen or break-
  fast room?
- Let the baby-sitter know what time you'll be home.
  If you are going to be late, be sure to call and let
  her or him know.

If you have some rules that can be broken and some
that are hard and fast, make the sitter aware of this.
Part of the fun of having Mom and Dad go out is that
a good sitter showers the children with lots of attention and lets them bend a rule here and there, so
be sure your sitter knows which ones are not to be
broken.

After you've used the sitter a number of times and
are sure you and the children are comfortable with

him or her, you can begin to plan longer evenings away, minimoons, and even your weeklong vacations.

I know it sounds like a lot of work, but it's worth it, and once you've established a routine with a regular sitter, everything will go like clockwork. Leaving your children with a baby-sitter gives you the time and privacy you and your mate need to be lovers again. The inhibitions that exist at home because of a lack of privacy disappear when you are away from the house. You and your mate will have the time and space you need to nurture your love for each other, and everyone, especially your children, will benefit from a home where love thrives.

OBSTACLE #2—YOU DON'T HAVE THE MONEY

I know some of you are reading this and saying to each other, "She must be crazy. We can't afford a baby-sitter for one night, let alone a weekend or a week." Well, I'm here to convince you that **you can't afford not to spend the money to get away alone together!** This is an investment in your future. Without this plan in place, there will be *no future* for the two of you as a happy couple. If you don't spend the money now on good times, such as a much-needed and deserved *temporary* escape *with* your mate for fun, relaxation, and lovemaking, I guarantee you'll be spending it later to pay for the bad times, such as a *permanent* escape *from* your mate, accompanied by divorce, anxiety, and tension. Believe me, it is infinitely cheaper to pay for a baby-sitter and a vacation than it is to pay for marriage counseling and a divorce attorney.

To help convince yourselves that what I say is true,

do the following exercise: Draw a line vertically down the center of a piece of paper, dividing it into two columns. At the top of the first column, write, "The Cost of Going on a Vacation Without the Children." Below that, put all the costs involved, such as child care, transportation, lodging, food, and anything else that you can think of. At the top of the second column, write, "The Cost of Not Going on a Vacation Without the Children." Below that, put down all the consequences you can think of that might result from neglecting your marriage. Here are a few suggestions:

- Missing out on feeling like lovers again
- Drifting apart
- Loss of intimacy
- Buildup of stress
- Nothing to look forward to
- Stress-induced illness
- Boredom
- Anger
- Forgetting how to talk to each other

You can't neglect your marriage without cheating your children, so be honest as you search your hearts for the damage that can result from putting your relationship last. Remember, just as a child can die from neglect, so can a marriage. Without the proper nurturing, your love for each other will shrivel up and die.

Clint, a former student of mine, recently took the time to write to me about some changes he's made in his marriage since he took my class. Clint and his wife have four children ranging in age from twelve to two. "When I thought about it, I realized that the amount of money we had to spend after the children came along was equivalent to what we had to spend before the children. The difference was that our marriage, our time alone together, went to the bottom of the list. Everything else came first. Before I took your class, the money went for the mortgage payment, utilities, insurance, medical bills, food, clothes, and lessons for the children. So, when it came time for fun for my wife and [me], I really believed there was no money left over. Let me fill you in on what I did immediately after your class. I started a 'Love Jar.' Now, before we put money aside for all the necessities, we take a small amount and put it in our Love Jar. We were amazed at how fast it added up. In just a few months we had saved enough to vacation at a dude ranch in Colorado for a week. It was the best time we'd had in years, and this mommy and daddy became lovers again. Thanks for putting us 'back in the saddle again.' "

Other students have reported that they, too, have started a love fund. Paul and Jean's marriage was already in trouble when Paul took my class. One of Jean's complaints was that they never got to spend any time away from the children. Paul wrote to tell me, ". . . for Jean's birthday I decorated a shoe box with gift wrap and used those stick-on letters you get from the stationery store to spell out 'Our minimoon box' on it. I wrote Jean a card telling her this was the last birthday we'd celebrate at home. From now on, we were going to put money aside in our minimoon box and every year she'll get to pick out where she wants to go. I just had to write and tell you that even though this was an IOU vacation for next year, Jean hasn't stopped telling her friends how excited she is."

In *Light Her Fire,* I carefully explained to my readers that women really need something to look forward to. That's why we love dates. I also emphasized that women are never completely relaxed and uninhibited in their own home. To a woman, home represents work. We are always aware of everything that needs to be done: the carpets that need to be vacuumed, the floors that need to be mopped, the clothes that need to be washed, the dinner that needs to be prepared, the furniture that needs to be dusted, the phone calls that need to be returned, the mail that has to be answered, and the children who need our attention. In case you haven't already figured it out, *this is not an environment that makes for a sex goddess!*

Women, listen to me. You must get out of that house!

Men, hear this now. You've got to get her out of the house!

You have to get away together where there are no distractions on a consistent basis. Heed my advice and watch the intimacy and sensuality come back into your relationship as you focus on each other and your only worry is "How can I please my lover?"

One of my students was a woman who was divorced from her children's father. She told me that the major problem in her marriage had been her husband's reluctance to leave the children for more than an occasional evening. He had a difficult childhood and an unrealistic notion of what "good parenting" should be. "Even when we went to marriage counseling, and the therapist offered to see us for a reduced fee if we would spend the money on a date or a weekend away together, my ex-husband balked at the idea. I hated the idea of breaking up the family, but hard as I tried, I just couldn't be a good wife and mother under those circumstances," my student lamented. "After thirteen years, I finally faced the reality that it wasn't going to get better. Maybe if we had both had access to this class, it could have been different," she concluded.

I love getting letters like the one I got from Jill. She wrote to tell me that she was very nervous about asking her friend Susan if she would be willing to watch Jill's children for a weekend in exchange for Jill doing the same for her. "Well," Jill wrote, "she was thrilled and thought it was a great idea. We started doing that a year ago, and every couple of months we give each other a look which says, 'It's time to do it again.' Then we decide who goes first.

"With the kids out of the house, my husband Bob and I have more fun using our own home, rather than an expensive hotel. I took your advice, and every weekend so far I've had a different theme. Last time I went with an Hawaiian theme. I made leis with tissue-paper flowers for us to wear around our necks and scented them lightly with a Plumeria oil. I borrowed a beautiful potted palm tree from my neighbor's patio and put it right in our bedroom. I had big, soft pillows on the floor and island music played on my stereo. I also bought a small hibachi so we could cook beef and chicken kabobs together. I filled a basket with tropical fruit and cut a fresh pineapple into chunks, which I hand-fed Bob as we toasted each other with Mai Tai cocktails. When Bob came home from work, I greeted him with your Ten-Second Kiss, dressed in a sarong I had made from a flowered print fabric. I had made him one too, and after he changed into it I placed the lei around his neck and handed him a cocktail. That was on Friday night. Saturday morning Bob brought me breakfast in bed and we made love all day. That evening we took a long walk, holding hands the whole time." Jill ended her letter by saying, "You're right. It doesn't have to take a lot of money to have a great weekend getaway with your mate. It just takes time, effort and creativity to be honeymooners for life."

Many couples sit around and wait for the time to come when they can afford to invest in their relationship. They tell themselves, "Someday, when we have enough money, we'll go away together." Well, while these couples fantasize about their *somedays*, couples like Jill and Bob are enjoying the pleasures that are available to them *today*. I realize that it's often difficult to make these kinds of changes. It raises all kinds of feelings in you, your children, and your spouse. Some of you may worry that your parents, who never took a vacation alone together in their entire lives, will disapprove. Some of you may feel guilty for wanting time away from your children. Just remind yourself that times have changed; we expect more than our parents did, and more is expected of us. Remind yourself that life is much more complex, and the need to have a lifetime affair with your mate is greater than it was in the past. Remind yourselves that your children need this as much as you do. Remind yourself that if you don't have an affair with your mate, someone else will. Most important of all, remind yourself that a shack can be a mansion when love lives there, and a palace can be a prison without love.

OBSTACLE #3—WE'RE TOO TIRED TO GO OUT

I know that some of you may feel that you don't have the energy it takes to get out of the house or plan a special weekend for the two of you. You're exhausted at the end of the day or the end of the week, and you still have a million things to do. Believe me when I tell you that no matter how tired and exhausted you are when you first leave the house, you'll return energized and happy that you went. When my children were little, I had a permanent baby-sitter lined up for every Saturday night. Inevitably, by Friday I'd start my inner dialogue, telling myself how exhausted I was and how I really didn't want to go out Saturday night. Sometimes I'd have the phone in my hand, ready to cancel the sitter, but there was another voice in my head, guiding me in another direction. It would say, "Do you really want to skip the one night of the week that you can be alone with your husband?" I knew that if I did skip it, we would feel distant from each other all next week. "Once you go, you'll be glad you did," my inner voice would nag me. I'd always go, although often reluctantly, and each time an amazing thing would happen. I always returned home with more energy than I'd had when I left.

My husband felt the same way. He had a demanding job and worked hard all week. He traveled a lot and really valued his time at home. He has told me that often he just wanted to sit in his recliner and "veg" out in front of the television on Saturday night, but he was always glad we went out. Both of us found that the more time we spent concentrating on each other, the more loved we felt. This had an energizing effect on us. We were able to think more clearly when we removed ourselves from the daily stresses that are a part of life, and best of all, we always got back in touch with the most important person in our lives—each other.

If being too tired is one of your excuses for not spending time with your mate, begin paying attention to your "self-talk." It's generally accepted in the psychological community that our subconscious mind, which controls our body and our physical and emotional responses, is programmed by our conscious mind. So, whatever we tell ourselves on a conscious level is what our subconscious, and our body, believes. How we feel—tired or energetic, listless or enthusiastic—is *mental*, not physical.

If you doubt this, imagine this scenario. You are so tired you can't keep your eyes open. You go to bed, and just as you're about to drift off, there's a knock at your front door. It's an old, dear friend who just happened to be in the neighborhood and decided to take a chance and see if you were home. Chances are something similar has happened to you sometime in the past. And you probably experienced a tremendous surge of energy. To continue our scenario, you'd get dressed and stay up half the night talking and not feel tired. How can this be? How can your body, which was dead tired a few minutes ago, now feel completely awake and energized? Because it got the following messages:

- Gee, I'm so excited.
- I'm so surprised and happy.
- There's so much catching up to do.
- I'll catch up on my sleep tomorrow.

If you allow yourself to send messages about how tired you are, you'll never have the motivation to go out. Instead, tell yourself:

- We're going to have a wonderful time.
- We're going to communicate on a deeper level.
- Our marriage really needs this.
- We really need a break from the kids.

- I'm going out with the most important person in my life.
- We have to stop being Mommy or Daddy and become lovers.

Once you're out the front door and it closes behind you, you'll take a deep breath, look into your lover's eyes, put your arms around each other, and begin walking away from the house, and you'll find that all of a sudden, out of nowhere, you'll feel the adrenaline begin to flow through your entire body.

OBSTACLE #4—WE DON'T HAVE THE TIME

If you already know what I'm going to say about this, it's a good sign. It means you're substituting my thoughts for your excuses. Just in case you're not sure, my response to this excuse is—*make the time!* These days, in over half the homes in America, both parents work outside the home. Even if one of the parents does stay home with the children, there are so many demands on a parent's time that there are never enough hours in the day or days in the week. PTA, lessons, sports, homework—all eat into the time parents have to spend with each other. To find time just to spend with your mate often seems like an impossibility. If that's the case in your family, then you may have to cut back on some of the activities you do with your children. Believe me, your children will not suffer if you are there:

- Six nights for them—one night for you and your mate

- Forty-eight weekends for them—four weekends for you and your mate
- Fifty-one weeks for them—one week for you and your mate

Paula and Dick have stopped using lack of time as an excuse. Paula says, "At least once a week Dick and I enjoy a candlelight dinner by ourselves." Paula also makes it a treat for their two children, who are four and seven years old. She takes them to the video store on their way home and lets the children pick out a video to watch that evening while she and Dick have dinner. "They know when I light the candles that it's Mommy and Daddy's special dinner. They settle down to watch their movie, and they know they are not to disturb us." If your meals always include the children, take one night out for a special dinner for just the two of you. You can dine at home or go to your favorite restaurant.

Finding time to be alone is always a challenge in the busy lives of parents, but something that is a challenge is often more interesting than something that's too easy. When you first got involved with your mate, you spent hours planning and dreaming about the time when you would be with your lover again. You would do anything to spend time with your mate—stay up all night, get up at the crack of dawn, whatever it took to have more time together. Finding time to be together was a challenge, but a welcome one. Now that you are parents, you have the same challenge. So face the challenge creatively and find new ways to spend time together.

Yes, it might take a little more arranging and planning and energy to be alone together now that you have children, but don't cheat yourselves out of the precious time when you can be lovers as well as parents just because you lack imagination or are afraid to try something new.

OBSTACLE #5—YOU REALLY DON'T FEEL ROMANTIC

If one of the reasons you don't want to go on a date, a weekend getaway, or a longer vacation with your mate is because you know your mate will expect romance and you don't feel romantic at this point in your life, you're not alone. Job pressures, the demands of raising children, the worries of everyday living—all take their toll in the romance department. Men and women alike go through periods when romance is the furthest thing from their mind. There are many times in every relationship where this is the case, but there is a simple, foolproof way to remedy the situation.

Earlier I talked about "self-talk," and how our subconscious mind is programmed based on the messages it gets from our conscious mind. If you are the kind of person who sends negative messages to your subconscious, then your reality will reflect those negative messages. Instead of telling yourself:

- I'm not a creative person,
- I don't have any imagination,
- I'm not a touchy-feely person,
- I always worry about making a fool of myself,
- I don't feel good about my body,
- I'm not much fun to be with,

simply make the messages positive:

- I *am* a creative person.
- I *have* a good imagination.
- I *love* touching and being touched.
- I *have* enough *confidence* to try new things.
- I *am* comfortable with my body.
- I *am* fun to be with.

As you change your negative self-talk to positive self-talk, reinforce the new messages by *acting as if* they are true. That's right. Pretend that you are the most romantic, witty, fun-loving, confident, sexy person in the world. If necessary, make believe that you are someone different from whom you really are. Then ask yourself, "How would I *act* and what would I do *if* I really felt this way about myself?"

Alma is a perfect example of someone who used this simple technique successfully. One night she came to class and said, "You know, after three kids, I've put on some weight. My husband says he thinks I look great, but I know I need to lose those last ten pounds. Anyway, I decided to try Ellen's suggestion. It's been a long time since I felt sexy, but I began to think about what I would do *if* I were sexy. That put me in the mood to buy a sexy new nightgown, which I modeled for my husband that night. He was thrilled. You know, it's amazing, but Ellen's right. Even though I started out just pretending I was sexy, the shopping, the anticipation, and Justin's positive reaction resulted in my actually feeling sexy. We ended up having a *very* romantic evening," Alma giggled.

One of the men who took "Light Her Fire," my class for men, admitted that the past year had been a very bad time for him financially. He had almost filed for bankruptcy and was working twelve-to-fourteen-hour days to save his business. He was almost home from work one evening when he remembered the new technique we had talked about in class. The last thing I feel is romantic and loving, he thought, but what would I do if I did? He turned the car around and drove to the supermarket, where he picked up a bouquet of flowers and a bottle of champagne. When he arrived home, he rang the front doorbell instead of going through the garage and in the back door, as he usually did. "When my wife answered the door, she was very surprised to see me standing there with flowers in one hand and champagne in the other," Carl said. Carl told her that her husband was too frustrated and tired to come home and had sent him as his replacement. His wife caught on right away, laughed, and said, "Boy, I sure could use the attention. Come on in." When Carl gave her a long, passionate kiss, his wife said, "Tell my husband to stay away for good. I like you better!"

Try this technique yourself, and you, too, will find that what starts out as a pretense becomes real. That's because *the subconscious mind doesn't know the difference between what's real and what's make-believe.* It reacts the same way to any message it gets from the conscious mind, whether it's negative or positive, real or pretend. This same technique can be used to improve your life, as well as your relationship.

- If you are basically a negative person and "doom and gloom" is your middle name, *act as if* you are a positive, optimistic person—one who makes everyone feel wonderful when they are with you.
- If you don't feel sexy or are shy and inhibited when it comes to sex, *act as if* you love your body, love sex, and are totally uninhibited.

- If you've lost that lovin' feeling for your mate, *act as if* you are involved in a mad, passionate love affair with him or her.
- If you are very insecure, *act as if* you are full of self-confidence.
- If you are shy and uncomfortable around people, *act as if* you are outgoing and assertive.

Once you *act the part, you will become the part.*

Sometimes a couple are so out of practice when it comes to being lovers that when they do finally take the opportunity to go away together for a romantic getaway, they're not sure how to make the event as idyllic as possible. The following tips will help you plan the perfect lovers' tryst.

Eleven Tips on How to Have a Romantic Evening in a Hotel Without the Children

1. Pack a red light bulb in your luggage. Without your partner's knowledge, replace the light bulb in the hotel room with your red light bulb. When he or she turns the light on, the room will be flooded with a soft red glow. Tell your mate, "Red is the color of love, and I wanted to fill the whole room with my love for you."

2. Put a rose in a plastic bag. While your mate is showering or soaking in the tub, scatter the petals of the rose on the sheets and pillows. When your mate sees the rose petals, tell him or her that you've always wanted to make love on a "bed of roses."

3. Order room service and, using no utensils, feed each other with your hands. Be prepared to ex-

perience anything from hilarious laughter to the joy you felt on your wedding day when you fed each other a slice of cake.

4. Plan on giving your partner a one-hour massage. There are some wonderful creams and lotions on the market that will help ease the tension and erase the cares and worries brought along on the trip.

5. Always request a room with a tub. If available, a Jacuzzi tub for two is the best.

6. Add bubble bath to your list of essential toiletries. On the evening of your choice, have a champagne toast to the two of you as you enjoy a bubble bath together.

7. Arrange to meet in the hotel lobby bar or restaurant. Pretend you are strangers meeting for the first time, who are wildly attracted to each other and can hardly wait to be alone.

8. Have an intimate dinner in your room. Ask the hotel to provide candles to add to a romantic atmosphere.

9. Bring along a book of beautiful poetry and read some of your favorite poems to your mate.

10. At the end of your stay, use the hotel stationery to write a love letter to your mate. While the memories are still fresh, tell him or her how much he or she means to you and how wonderful it has been spending these precious hours alone together.

11. Of course, don't forget to bring along my wonderful game, "How to Host a Romantic Evening." By creating an exotic mood, you can take a journey of the mind without leaving your room. This game helps you focus on what you enjoy about each other and lets you use your imagination to

put fireworks and communication in your relationship. If you have a problem finding it, you can
write to me at the address at the back of the book.

Admittedly, there are obstacles to be overcome in
order to stay lovers after the children come into your
life. As I've demonstrated in these pages, these obstacles can be looked at as challenges, and you can enjoy
the challenge instead of dreading it. Very few of us
are thrilled when the alarm rings at 6:00 A.M., but we
get up because we want to keep our job. At work,
there are many things we may not want to do, such
as working overtime or being pleasant to an obnoxious boss, but we do them to get ahead or to keep
from getting fired. When someone's needs are not
met, that's often what happens. We fire our current
mate and find a substitute who will fulfill our needs.
Whether it's an affair or a divorce doesn't really matter. If you don't have an affair with your mate, it's
only a matter of time until you are replaced by someone who is smart enough not to make excuses.

SEIZE THE MOMENT

I asked hundreds of couples who are still in love with
each other and whose children are happy and well
adjusted the secret of their wonderful relationship. Although each couple may say it a little differently, the
bottom line is always the same. *Their relationship has
been, is, and always will be their top priority.* Even couples with five or six children seized the chance to
make love when the baby took a nap or when the
older children were in school. These happy couples
are the ones who would hire a baby-sitter so they

could go for a walk or have a romantic dinner alone. They are the ones who would trade baby-sitting with a neighbor so they could spend a weekend alone together. As the children got older, these lovers taught the children to respect their privacy when their bedroom door was closed. These were not terrible, selfish parents. On the contrary, theirs was the healthy, normal behavior of a couple who respected their own sexuality and valued the romantic love they shared.

Even though the ideas I've discussed here may seem farfetched to you at first, they work. Just be focused, positive, and committed. As some very wise person once said:

Whatever you vividly imagine, ardently desire, sincerely believe, and enthusiastically act upon MUST inevitably come to pass.

ASSIGNMENT #3

Becoming a Better Parent

1. Sit down with your children and explain that Mom and Dad are starting a new program. Tell them that from now on, one night a week is going to be date night for Mommy and Daddy, and that every three months you'll be going away for a weekend together. Tell them that once a year you're going to take a one-week vacation alone together. Let them know it's very important to have adult time to do adult things that aren't much fun for kids.
2. Involve the children in hiring a baby-sitter. Tell them their opinion of those you choose as potential sitters is very important to you.
3. Let the children help you put together a special

loose-leaf notebook (so you can add and take out pages) for the sitter. Let them decorate it. Keep all the important phone numbers in this notebook, along with all the special rules of the house. Write each rule at the top of a page and let the children draw a picture to illustrate that rule. For example, if the children are allowed to eat only in the kitchen or family room, write that rule at the top of a page and have them draw a picture of themselves sitting at the table, eating. If your children are old enough, they can write the rule on the page themselves, as well as drawing a picture. If they don't want to draw, they can look through magazines and cut out appropriate pictures to paste on the page.

Becoming a Better Partner

1. Begin calling your mate a pet name. Let it become a playful way of relating as lovers.
2. Begin greeting each other with your heart and soul. Institute the Ten-Second Kiss.
3. Make a commitment to the "Lovers' Program." Hire a baby-sitter and go out one night this week.
4. Begin planning your minimoons and seven-day vacations, so you'll have something exciting to look forward to. Start a vacation folder, and fill it with pictures and articles you find in magazines or the travel section of the Sunday newspaper. Visit travel agencies and collect brochures to some of the places you've always dreamed about. These activities will give you and your mate some great ideas and will give you something to talk about when you are alone together.
5. Schedule a romantic weekend getaway.
6. Schedule your one-week vacation sometime soon.

Four

GUILT: A MOTHER'S DISEASE

GUILTY NO MATTER WHAT YOU DO

If you are a mother, you are familiar with the concept of guilt. Guilt is the feeling you have whenever you aren't feeling pressured, rushed, stressed, anxious, worried, resentful, angry, or tired. In other words, guilt is the feeling women have when they are relaxed, enjoying their favorite leisure-time activity, and fulfilling their own needs.

Over the years, I have found that while guilt is a feeling experienced by almost everyone at one time or another, the difference between a mother's guilty feelings and a father's guilty feelings has to do with frequency and intensity. When I asked my students, "Is guilt an emotion you experience?" most of the men answered "occasionally," "sometimes," or "once in a while," while women answered "every day," "all the time," and "constantly." It is my belief that guilt is an inherited disease, one passed down from mother to daughter, generation after generation. I have found that women, especially mothers, feel guilty no matter what they do. If they stay home and bake cookies, they feel guilty because they aren't "fulfilling" themselves with a challenging career or contributing to the family coffers. If they work full time, they feel guilty because they aren't fully involved with their children. They can't be PTA president, Girl Scout leader, and soccer-team secretary if they have to be on the job eight hours a day. And working part time is sometimes the greatest guilt inducer of all—leaving a mother feeling bad for giving only half an effort to the kids and half an effort to her job. It doesn't seem to matter whether women have a full-time job, a part-time job, or no job at all. They all feel guilty.

Today's women work for a variety of reasons. Many work because the family can't make it on one paycheck. Some must work because they are single and are the sole support of their children. Others choose to work because they enjoy being independent. For many women, a job provides mental stimulation, a creative outlet, and a sense of worth. Still others work because they know if they stay home, they'll drive themselves and everyone around them crazy.

Whatever the reason, millions of women are managing to balance career, marriage, and family. Most are doing a wonderful job. Unfortunately, a vast number of women feel too guilty to enjoy what they've accomplished. Nadine said, "Although I love my job and wouldn't dream of giving it up, I feel guilty for shortchanging my children. I have a heavy travel schedule, and I miss major developments and events in their lives because I spend so much time away from home."

Ironically, it's not just working women who feel guilty. Charlene confessed that she sometimes feels guilty for being "just" a housewife and not a career woman. "I'm very fortunate to be able to stay home with the children, and I really love it, but sometimes I feel guilty about not accomplishing enough at home," she said.

Even Marlene, who works part time, feels guilty. "Nothing I do gets my full attention. I feel like I'm doing a disservice to my employer, who wants me to come back to work full time, and I worry that my children are being cheated as well. There just doesn't seem to be a happy medium," she sighed.

No matter how liberated women like to think they've become, most of the men I talk to still see themselves as the person primarily responsible for supporting the family. As Craig pointed out one night, society still points the finger of blame at the male if a couple wind up penniless and on welfare. Since the male's belief is that his first responsibility is to earn a living, if he does help with the cooking, cleaning, and child care, he's likely to think he's a terrific husband and father. After all, he's doing so much more than his father did. On the other hand, most women still see themselves as the primary caretaker of the house and children, and if the house is a mess or the children are unruly, it's usually she who takes the blame. Seldom, if ever, do you hear the father accused of keeping a messy house or not handling the children properly. In fact, just recently my husband and I were at a restaurant where a child at the next table was misbehaving. The waitress who took our order said to us, "Boy, there's a mother who can't control her own child." I found that to be an interesting comment since *both* parents were with the child. It's comments like this that lead women to believe that somewhere out there is this perfect mom who has a perfectly behaved child, in a perfectly maintained home, married to a perfectly contented husband—and who has achieved all this while successfully pursuing a high-paying, challenging, and fulfilling career. Unrealistic expectations such as these make a woman's already complicated life even more stressful.

THERE'S NO SUCH THING AS SUPERWOMAN

I believe that a women can have it all and do it all.

I just don't believe that we can have it all and do it all *all at the same time*. The picture we have of the perfect wife, the perfect mother, and the perfect career woman is pure fiction and does not exist anywhere but in our imaginations.

In the many years that I've been teaching and lecturing, I've met thousands of women, but I've never met one who had a successful career, was a terrific mother, and had a wonderful marriage *all at the same time*. While I do believe you can experience success in all of these areas, I don't believe it is possible to experience success in all three areas *simultaneously*. I believe that anyone who says she can is a liar.

To live life successfully, you must make choices. The happiest, most contented women I know are the ones who have examined themselves, their situation, and their needs and decided what their priorities are. Women who blindly follow the paths their mothers took, or who succumb to the dictates of society and their peers, may be making decisions that are not right for them. Just because your mother stayed home and was a full-time mom doesn't mean you should. On the other hand, just because your college roommate is now a corporate executive and you're a stay-at-home mom doesn't mean you're a failure. The true measure of success in anything is the sense of happiness and fulfillment it brings you.

Some women choose to make their career their first priority. Erma, a thirty-eight-year-old gynecologist, had two children—an eight-year-old and a six-year-old. She said, "I used to drive myself crazy trying to be the perfect wife, the perfect mother, and the perfect doctor—a goal I finally realized was impossible. After taking Ellen's course, I realized that the happier I was, the happier my husband and children would be. I knew that I was most happy when I was helping other women, and I decided that by concentrating on my career, I would be giving my family the best wife and mother possible."

At the time she took my class, being a good wife was Emily's first priority. "For the past few years, I've been buried by diapers. Having three children all under the age of five has consumed all of my time. It was my husband Harold's idea that we both take your class and concentrate on each other for a while. We had begun to feel like strangers. Now it's time to get back to being a wife."

For Marjorie, becoming a full-time mother was a priority. "I missed my daughter's first two birthdays because I was out of town on business," she said regretfully. "I kept asking myself why I was doing this. Finally, I decided that I want to stay home and be with my daughter for a while. I know I'm lucky to have the choice, and I intend to make the most of it," she said.

If you are concentrating on a career, you cannot keep your house immaculate and do all the cooking the way your mother did. If you are concentrating on your children, you cannot expect to rise to the top of your profession, and if you concentrate on being a great partner, you'll have to exclude your children some of the time (especially if you take my advice).

If you will just stop trying to be "superwife," "supersuccess," and "supermom" all at the same time, you'll feel less guilty and enjoy your life more.

A HEALTHIER OUTLOOK ON GUILT

I have yet to meet a man who feels guilty because he isn't a super father, a super husband, and highly successful at earning a living, all at the same time. It's much more typical for men to have realistic expectations of themselves than it is for them to stress out trying to be perfect in several roles at once. One father I know took custody of his two children when he and his wife divorced. As soon as arrangements had been completed and he was finally the full-time caretaker of his children, he met with his boss.

"Now that I'm a single father," he said, "my children come first. I may be late to work, I may take long lunch hours, I may leave early, and sometimes I may not come in at all," he said. "It just depends on what my children need on any given day."

Even if they were in a position to do it, how many women do you know who could take that stand at work without feeling extremely guilty?

While most men I've spoken to may feel there's room for improvement in one or more of these areas, they certainly aren't plagued by guilt. Leigh said, "Sure, I feel bad sometimes about the long hours I work, but I provide a good living and a comfortable lifestyle for my family. Could I be a better father? Absolutely, but then my son wouldn't have the material rewards of my labor, such as owning his own car and having his college expenses paid."

Rocky said, "I think I'm a pretty good father. I certainly feel I'm involved in my son's activities. At times I wish that I earned more money, but we have enough to get by, and we enjoy doing things as a family."

Greg admits that there's room for improvement in the romance department. "I may not be a Don Juan," he says, "but I love my wife and kids a great deal. I go out there and work hard every day to earn a living because I want them to have the best that life has to offer."

Sorry, ladies, but on the subject of guilt, most men have a healthier outlook and can teach us a great deal.

WHAT DO YOU SAY TO YOURSELF WHEN YOU FEEL GUILTY?

I wish I could tell you how to live guilt-free, but I can't. Knowing women as I do, I know that you will always feel some degree of guilt. The best that I can do is show you how to have *less* guilt. The first step to feeling less guilty is to talk back to your guilty thoughts. Every time you feel guilty, replace your guilty thoughts with thoughts that are more encouraging and supportive—thoughts such as:

I haven't done anything wrong or bad. It's okay to respect my own needs.

Putting your needs before your child's needs is not a reason to feel guilty. The mother who sacrifices her own happiness for the sake of her children is the epitome of a martyred mother who saddles her children with a lifetime load of guilt. Think of it this way: If you meet your needs, you're saving your children from feeling guilty for depriving you.

Lena said that because of the class, she and her husband decided to go out on a date for the first time since her fifteen-month-old daughter was born. She said, "We had a wonderful time, but when we came home, my daughter was awake and crying. The babysitter told us that thirty minutes after we left, our daughter woke up and had not stopped crying the entire time. The sitter had tried everything but couldn't get Kimberly back to sleep. A wave of guilt swept over me. How could I have done this to my 'poor' helpless baby? But then I remembered what we had talked about in class. I told myself that I had done nothing wrong. I really needed to spend time with my husband. I really needed to have adult conversation. I really needed to feel like a wife again, instead of just a mother."

I was really proud of Lena, because she was able to replace her guilty feelings with more supportive thoughts. She made the decision to feel guilty, but continued to go out on a regular basis with her husband. The last I heard, her daughter had finally adjusted to the baby-sitter, and Lena and her husband have a new closeness as a couple. Although Lena's child had every right to be upset at the unavailability of her mother, Lena also had every right to pay attention to her own needs.

I'm only human, and therefore I will make mistakes. Each mistake is an opportunity to learn and increase my level of awareness.

All of us make mistakes, and mothers are no exception. No matter how hard you try, you will never be perfect, but in some areas mothers are especially susceptible to guilt if they make a mistake. Our child's health and safety is one of those areas. "How could any mother allow her child to come to harm or fail to protect her child?" we reason. It happens—and feeling guilty doesn't change it.

When my daughter Tiffany was five years old, she and her six-year-old sister were fooling around, giving each other piggyback rides using my bed as a launching pad. I was busy with a long-distance phone call. When I heard Tiffany crying and yelling, "Mommy, Mommy, I fell and broke my arm," I just yelled from the other room, "Stop fooling around," and continued with my phone call. That night she complained that her arm hurt and kept saying it was broken, but I dismissed it as a bump and did nothing. The next morning, I was horrified when I saw her arm. It was black and blue and swollen to twice its normal size. I took her to the doctor immediately and, sure enough, her arm was broken and had to be put in a cast.

I was so ashamed. In an effort to make me feel better, the doctor told me that his own son had walked around with a broken arm for three days before the doctor had taken him seriously. It didn't help me to hear that. I walked around feeling guilty for months. I kept blaming myself for not listening to Tiffany when she said her arm was broken. Over and over, I kept saying, "How could I have done that? I'm such a terrible mother." Eventually, I guess I felt I had punished myself enough, and at that point my *thoughts* are what actually changed. You see, the situation was still the same. My daughter had broken her arm, and it had to be put in a cast. Nothing I could do or say would change that. The only thing that could change were my thoughts regarding what happened. Finally, I began to talk to myself in a more supportive, caring way. I was able to say, "You *are* a good mother. You are also a human being who made a mistake. You've learned from this never to ignore your child's self-diagnosis or pain again." In fact, that's when I came up with my scale of one to ten. From then on, whenever the children felt pain or didn't feel good, they'd tell me, on a scale of one to ten, how much pain they were in or how sick they felt.

In the years since Tiffany broke her arm, I have learned that when you blame yourself, what you are really saying is "I didn't do as much as I *should* or *could* have done." *Blame* is always based on new information that you didn't have at the time. If I had known my daughter's arm was broken, I would have acted differently. I really didn't think that was the case at the time.

It's okay for me to take my own time and work at my own pace. I'm not in competition with anyone else.

A student named Eva said that this is the thought that helped her the most. "I just gave birth three months ago, and I'm still very uncomfortable. Christopher weighed almost ten pounds, and it was a very difficult birth. I can still feel my stitches. On top of my discomfort, I felt a lot of guilt. All my friends have told me how giving birth was no big deal. They went back to work after six weeks and are having super sex. I kept saying to myself, 'You are such a wimp. Everyone else gives birth, and it's a breeze.' After this class, I changed my thoughts to, I don't care what anyone else does. This is my body, and it hurts. In time, it will heal, and everything will be okay. I'll take as much time as I need, and I won't worry about what other people have done. I repeated this over and over, and you know what? I finally believe it!"

It's important to think about how I really feel. It's okay to say no when I don't want to do something.

Every December, Cecillia's entire family came from the Midwest to sunny California to celebrate Christmas. In September, she would get depressed just thinking about everything she had to do to accommodate everyone. The year she took my class, Cecillia's husband won a contest at work. The prize was a one-week cruise right smack in the middle of December. Cecilia was distressed, because there was no way she could take this trip *and* prepare for her family's arrival. She had to make a choice—did she want to go on the cruise with her husband or stay home and continue the family tradition? She had plenty of time to decide, so I just had her repeat over and over, "It's important to think about how I really feel. What do I really want to do?"

Mind you, this was a woman who hadn't paid any attention to her own feelings for many, many years. After several nights of tormented sleep, Cecillia decided she definitely wanted the cruise. When she called her sister to tell her the news, her sister's reaction was just as Cecillia expected.

"Well, what are we all supposed to do about Christmas?" her sister asked.

"I don't know," said Cecillia. "Since I've done all

the planning for the past eight years, I guess you'll have to talk to each other and make new plans." Cecillia told the class that it felt wonderful to acknowledge her own feelings for the first time in a very long time.

My parents did what they thought was right for them, but what was right for them is not necessarily right for me. It's okay for me to do things differently.

Tammy said every time her husband offered to help her with the dishes, she felt guilty. Barbara felt guilty when her husband offered to help with dinner. Both women realized that their mothers always insisted that their fathers and brothers stay out of the kitchen. They had heard their mothers say, "This is woman's work." Many women feel guilty because they do things differently than their mothers did. Even though our mothers may be thousands of miles away, or even deceased, we can still hear their voices in our head. One woman said, "My mother would turn over in her grave if she knew I don't make the bed every morning. I can still hear her criticizing someone we knew because she didn't make her bed. 'That woman can barely function—why, she doesn't even make her bed in the morning,' she'd say."

Audrey acknowledged that although she loved her job, she felt guilty. "Every day, when I drop my son off at the day-care center, I feel guilty. My mother was shocked when I went back to work after the baby was born. I hear her voice every day saying, 'I didn't work while you were growing up. A child needs his mother.' " Audrey had to learn how to fight back those thoughts by replacing them with new ones. She

reported having a much better week when she replaced her guilty feelings with positive thoughts. "I
love my job," she told herself. "It's taken me a long
time to achieve what I have, and it feels good. I'm a
wonderful mother who loves her child as well as her
job. My child sees a fulfilled woman with a healthy
self-esteem. Just because my mother stayed home
doesn't mean it was right or that I should, too."

We are all entitled to be different from our parents.
Our happiness depends on our ability to think for
ourselves. We must be free to make decisions based
on what we feel is important and necessary to us.

*I'm not responsible for someone else's happiness. They are
happy or unhappy depending on their own thoughts and
how they interpret a given situation.*

Christine's mother was driving her crazy. She called
every day to let Christine know how lonely, sad, depressed, and tired she was. Try as she would, Christine could not make her mother feel happy. Over and
over, Christine would reassure her mother that she
was loved very much by Christine and by her grandchildren, but no matter what Christine said or did, she
continued to have a "poor me" attitude. "I'm getting
depressed myself," said Christine, "and I don't have
the energy it takes anymore to listen to her negativity." I had Christine repeat the above thought over
and over. Gradually, she came to understand that she
truly wasn't responsible for her mother's happiness.
Christine mustered up her courage and called her
mother. She told her that she was too depressing to
talk to every day, and that she needed to "get a life"
(her words, not mine). She also asked her mother not

to call until she had something pleasant to talk about. As Christine expected, her mother was very angry and insulted. After a two-week silence, Christine's mother finally called and, much to Christine's surprise, actually apologized.

"I've been thinking a lot about what you said," her mother admitted, "and I know I feel sorry for myself much too much. You have your own problems. You certainly don't need to deal with mine, too. I want you to know I've joined a bridge club, and I've decided to sign up for some adult-education classes."

Christine said she couldn't believe her ears. "This stuff really works," she said, laughing.

It's okay to do something just for me. I am entitled to take time out for myself.

One of the homework assignments I routinely give in my women's class is to do something selfish during the week and report on it in class. One of my students, Sue, said something the week after she had completed her assignment that I never forgot. "I've always said, with a three-year-old and a five-year-old and a part-time job, 'I never *have* a moment to myself.' After this week's assignment, I realize that I never *take* a moment for myself. I'm so busy giving the kids their bath that I forgot how wonderful it feels to take a bath myself. On Saturday, my husband agreed to keep the kids occupied while I indulged in selfish pleasure. I purchased a bath pillow, a soothing New Age music tape, bubble-bath oils, a novel I've been wanting to read, and some nice herb tea. I can't remember ever feeling so relaxed. I soaked in that tub for over an hour, reading and sipping my tea. When I finally forced myself out of the tub, I tweezed my eyebrows and polished my fingernails and toenails. I intend to keep this as a weekly routine. Yes, I felt guilty, but as I soaked in that tub, I kept repeating, 'I'm worth it!' "

When my first book, *Light His Fire*, was published, I was scheduled for a three-week book tour across the United States. As it turned out, I needed to continue for an extra week. I really enjoyed every moment of the tour. The television shows, the radio interviews, the beautiful hotel accommodations, the wonderful people I met in every city were all very exciting to me. I also felt a tremendous amount of guilt for leaving my husband and fifteen-year-old son on their own for so long. When I called to tell my son that I'd be gone an extra week, he said something that touched me deeply and brought tears to my eyes.

"You've been such a great mom for all fifteen years of my life," he said. "Do you really think that one month is going to make any difference? You've worked so hard for this, and you deserve to enjoy yourself."

I can't tell you how wonderful he made me feel or how many times I've replayed his statement in my head.

Almost all women find it difficult to put their needs ahead of their own children's needs. As children, we were taught that it was wrong to be selfish or to think of ourselves first. I can even remember believing it was wrong to vote for yourself in a school election! The idea that you must always think of others first becomes so ingrained that once you become a mother, you become self-"less." Do yourself, and everyone you love, a favor. Learn to be selfish once in a while. At least half an hour each day, do something just for yourself. Try to remember that the more relaxed you are, the more patience you'll have with your children. In addition to the everyday stresses that we all experience, children can be very draining. You must replenish yourself so you have more to give to your family. Treat yourself with kindness, warmth, respect, and love. Why? Because you deserve it!

NO PERMISSION NEEDED

Children know exactly how to make you feel guilty and get what they want. They are the masters of this game. Children are very self-centered and believe that the whole world should revolve around them. It's up to you, as a parent, to teach them that this is not the case. If you are waiting for your children's permission to have an evening of entertainment without them or to go away on a vacation that doesn't include them, forget it! You'll be old and gray before it happens. In the film *This Is My Life*, actress Julie Kavner says, "You give kids a choice, their mother in the next room on the verge of suicide versus their mother in Hawaii in ecstasy, they'll pick suicide in the next room, believe me."

Children do not know what's good for them: You do. I know they want you home all the time, but they also want McDonald's every night for dinner. So, in spite of what they want, the last thing they need is unhappy parents who sacrifice everything for the sake of the child.

KICK THE WORRY HABIT

I have found that guilt and worry seem to go hand in hand. People who feel guilty a lot worry a lot. Guilt is feeling bad about something you are saying, doing, or feeling in the present or something you said, did, or felt in the past. Worry is the feeling that something bad is going to happen in the *future*.

Neither guilt nor worry change anything. They just keep you upset and unhappy. They are feelings, not facts. As I see it, worry is nothing more than a picture of the future that you don't want to happen. Suppose that your worst nightmare were to become a reality. That means you would have to go through it twice: once in your imagination as you worry about it, and again when it occurs.

For example, if your son or daughter is out late and hasn't called, you begin to worry that your child has been in an accident. If that actually happened, you would have gone through that horrible experience twice, once in your mind and once in reality. In fact, worry can often become a self-fulfilling prophecy. Perhaps you are the jealous type, who worries constantly that your husband will leave you for another woman. Your worry and jealous nature could actually cause your worst fear to come to pass. Because of your fear, you are suspicious and jealous. You constantly accuse your husband unfairly. He becomes sick of your jealousy. One day he meets a woman who is loving to him and . . . well, you know the rest of the story.

Another example might be that you learn you are pregnant. You are very happy, but then you begin to worry about whether your marriage will last. After all, so many of your friends are divorced. Not only will you ruin the happiness of the present with your depressing picture of the future, you might begin to act out your worry in such a way as to actually destroy your marriage.

Remember, the mind can't hold two thoughts at the same time. When a negative thought pops into your head about the future, fight back and change the picture to something positive. For example:

- Your husband is an hour late arriving home from work, and he hasn't called. You worry that he's been in an accident or is having a rendezvous with another woman.
  Instead, picture him arriving home safely and having a good explanation.
- You're up for a promotion, but you're worried that your colleague will get the promotion instead of you.
  Imagine yourself jumping for joy as your boss congratulates you on your promotion.
- Your entire family is traveling one thousand miles to spend the Thanksgiving holiday with you. You're worried that the turkey will be dry and the gravy will be lumpy.
  Visualize everyone sitting at the table enjoying the feast you prepared and raving about the delicious, moist turkey.
- You've just gotten a note that your child's teacher wants to set up a parent-teacher conference with you. You're worried that the teacher is going to tell you that your child is nothing but trouble and you are not raising him well.
  Imagine the teacher smiling at you and complimenting you on what a wonderful child you have.

The point is, I don't want you to create negative energy. Instead, create positive energy by creating a positive picture of the future. That way, if something awful should happen in the future, at least you'll only experience it *once*.

In *Julius Caesar*, Shakespeare writes:

> Cowards die many times before their deaths;
> The valiant never taste of death but once.

Don't be a coward by dying a thousand deaths. Be a hero to your mate, your children, and yourself by relinquishing worry for a positive outlook.

FEEL THE GUILT AND DO IT ANYWAY

When we deny our own feelings, we feel angry, resentful, and bitter. When we allow ourselves to do and have what we really want, although we may feel guilty, we also feel happy, excited, and affectionate. If you deprive yourself in order to avoid feeling guilty, everyone suffers from your anger and resentment. If you treat yourself well, on the other hand, the only person affected by your guilt will be you.

Personally, I think it would take years to get rid of my guilt, so I've decided to just feel the guilt and do it anyway, and I've taught thousands of guilty women to do the same.

We all laughed one night when Ava told the following story:

"My husband had been away on business for almost three weeks. I had to pick him up at the airport, and I decided to welcome him home with a naughty surprise. I wore my raincoat—and nothing else! I was totally naked underneath. Talk about guilt! When I was a child, my mother had always admonished me to wear clean underwear every day, so that if I was ever in an accident, the doctors and nurses would know I was a refined person. I got to giggling on my way to the airport as I imagined my mother's reaction to my state of 'undress.' I could just see the shocked look on her face as I asked, 'Well, Mom, what do you think the doctors and nurses would think if they saw me now?' "

Tina, a woman in her late fifties and a graduate of my class, wrote to tell me that she finally did what she's wanted to do for many years: She had a complete face-lift. "Until you covered the subject of guilt in class, I never would have had the courage to do it," she wrote. "My mother was a very plain woman who never wore makeup and who wouldn't have dreamed of coloring her hair. But I have always wanted to look as young as possible and have used everything commercially available to do so. However, there comes a time when cosmetics just don't do the job anymore, but I couldn't justify the money it would cost to indulge in a face-lift. It felt too selfish. After your class, I realized that I didn't have to justify it. We could afford it, so I decided to feel the guilt and do it anyway. I love the new me, and my husband and kids think I look fantastic. Thanks for giving me the guts to do what I wanted to do."

Ashley went on a vacation with her husband, leaving her four children in the capable hands of her sister.

"If it weren't for your tapes," she wrote, "I wouldn't have dreamed that this vacation would have been possible in a million years. After I listened to them, I realized that half our friends are divorced or miserable in their relationships. I felt very guilty putting our airline tickets on a charge card but, hey, I wanted to go to Hawaii while I can still water-ski, scuba-dive, wear a bikini, and make passionate love to my husband. I sure felt guilty, but I did it anyway."

How about you? What do you think would give you pleasure?

THE PLEASURE PRINCIPLE

I consider pleasure to be a necessity—not a luxury. Just as you plan for other parts of your life, you have to plan for those leisure activities that will give you pleasure. You put a doctor's appointment on your calendar, you put a dentist's appointment on your calendar, you schedule your car maintenance, and hopefully by now you schedule sex on your calendar. Now you need to schedule a selfish, pleasurable activity for yourself. I've already established the fact that regardless of what you do or don't do, you're going to feel guilty. So, feel the guilt and do it anyway! The following are some of the ways women have indulged in "selfish pleasure," while feeling very guilty!

- Take a day off from work without being sick or having to care for a sick child. Do it with the intent of staying in bed, watching television, and eating whatever you crave. When your husband and children come home and ask, "What did you do all day?" you can say with a smile, "Nothing."
- If you are a stay-at-home mom, hire a baby-sitter for several hours a week prior to deciding what you'll do with the free time. You don't need a "socially acceptable" reason for leaving the kids. First free up your time, and then decide what to do with it.
- Buy something just for yourself. It can be an entire

outfit or just a pretty new scarf. As a mother, you are always buying for your children. Give yourself permission to be a top priority. Your children benefit when you are feeling and looking your best.

- Make it a habit to take fifteen minutes in the morning and fifteen minutes in the evening to do relaxation exercises, including deep breathing and meditation. It will clear your mind, give you more energy, and help you relax.

- Invest in an answering machine. Most women feel they always have to answer the phone. After all, "What if it's an emergency?" With an answering machine, you don't have to answer the phone, and you don't have to return calls if you are busy or don't feel like it. Leave a message on the machine that lets people know you are busy and that you'll get back to them as soon as you have some free time. (That could be next week!) If it's an emergency, you'll hear the message and can react accordingly. Otherwise, you can return the call when you feel like it.

- Rent a real "tearjerker" of a movie. Nothing relieves stress like a good cry. Forget trying to get a family movie for the kids or one that pleases your mate. Instead of popcorn, buy a box of tissues and indulge yourself.

- Make regular appointments to see your doctor. Mothers get so busy with their children's doctors' appointments that they forget about themselves. You don't need anything wrong to have a checkup. Early detection of a serious medical condition could save your life, and learning that you are healthy makes you feel good and relieves stress.

- Get a nice, long massage. It's worth every penny. You'll feel as if you died and went to heaven.

- Have a professional manicure and pedicure. Your hands and feet should be pampered. After all the work they do every day, they need to be soaked, massaged, and beautiful.
- Network with other women whose situation is similar to yours. Whether you are a full-time mother or are combining a career with motherhood, it always helps to share your frustrations and triumphs with other women.
- Call up a few of your girlfriends and plan a ladies' night out. You can really feel guilty by splurging on a limousine and sharing the cost.
- Join a gym and stick to a regular workout schedule. You'll find that regular exercise reduces stress and makes you feel good about yourself, as well as improving your physical condition. Between trips to the gym, the new funk workouts are fun and energizing and can be done at home.
- Attend a fashion show with the intent of buying something for yourself.
- Schedule a luncheon with a friend and gossip, gossip, gossip. If you work, you can still do it by taking an extended lunch hour. Yes, I know you'll feel guilty.
- Schedule a makeover. Most large department stores offer a complete morning or afternoon of pampering. A facial, new hairdo, and new makeup will boost your self-esteem.
- Get started on a hobby. Select something that you've always wanted to do or you used to do before having children. It could be flying lessons, gourmet cooking, music lessons, painting, writing, or anything that allows you freedom of expression.
- Spend some time every day reading the newspaper, a novel, a self-help book, or a magazine. Anything

that relaxes your body and stimulates your mind
will do. You'll feel (and be) more interesting.

- Schedule time to soak in the bathtub. Buy a bath
  pillow, candles, soothing music, bath oils, and whatever else will help you soak your cares away. Just
  remember to chant, "I'm worth it. I deserve it."

- Find a beautiful spot and take a long walk. The
  woods, a park, the beach, even window-shopping in
  the mall will relax your mind and energize your
  body.

- Take a tea break. Buy some nicely scented herb teas
  and a pretty tea service. In the afternoon, take a tea-
  tray set with a cup of tea, a flower in a vase, and a
  cookie and sit on the patio or in front of the fire and
  daydream for a few minutes.

- Go to church, synagogue, or other place of worship.
  If you're a religious person, going alone to a chapel
  for a few minutes of quiet prayer can restore your
  peace of mind.

Feel free to add whatever selfish pleasure you can
think of that would help you stay centered. Just remember that the happier and more fulfilled you are,
the more you have to give to your mate and children.
If we ever meet, I want to see you smile and hear you
say, "Boy, am I feeling guilty these days."

ASSIGNMENT #4

Becoming a Better Parent

1. Help your children grow up to be healthy, fulfilled
   adults by not making them feel guilty now. Stop if
   you catch yourself making statements like:

"Shame on you."

"If you loved Mommy, you'd . . ."

"You'll give me a heart attack yet."

"You make my blood pressure go up."

"How could you embarrass me like that?"

"What will the neighbors think?"

"I sacrificed my life for you."

"I'm stuck in this house because of you."

2. Help your children understand your need to spend time on yourself with the following analogy:

Imagine Mommy as a large pitcher filled to the brim with red liquid. The red liquid is love. Now, picture some empty glasses. The empty glasses are Daddy, you kids, my friends, our neighbors — anybody who needs my love or requires something of me. As Mommy takes care of each of these people, imagine that some of her love liquid is being poured into each glass. What happens to the pitcher (Mommy) as she fills up everyone else's love cup? It (Mommy) becomes empty. And when Mommy's empty, she has nothing else to give. By being good to herself, Mommy refills her "love cup" (the pitcher).

3. When you are eating dinner together, share a little about your job, as well as asking about the children's day.

4. Invite your children to see you at work. Children are less likely to make you feel guilty if they know what you are doing during the day.

Becoming a Better Partner

1. Pay attention to your guilty feelings. Replace your guilty thought with a more supportive and encouraging thought.

2. Instead of trying to achieve perfection in every area of your life, relax a little and settle for "close

enough." You'll be happier, and so will your mate.

3. Combat worry by replacing your catastrophic thoughts with a more positive picture of the future.

4. Feel the guilt and indulge in selfish pleasure anyway. Schedule time for yourself. Let your mate reap the rewards of a happier, more fulfilled woman.

Five

LET THE FIREWORKS BEGIN

SEX IS A DECISION

Couples with no children have the luxury of enjoying uninterrupted conversation, romantic candlelight dinners, lazy weekends, and unhurried sex, but when there are children to consider, a romantic interlude usually must be planned. From the very beginning, a newborn baby interferes with your freedom in every way. Besides depriving you of sleep, an infant deprives you of the liberty to come and go as you please, or to do what you want to do—when you want to do it. Believe it or not, there can be a distinct advantage to this lack of freedom. Since you are parents, you must be more flexible, creative, and focused in meeting your needs. In fact, the older your children, the more flexible, creative, and focused you have to become. By learning to be creative, you'll be forced to find new and exciting ways to be lovers.

Although most couples like to think sex was spontaneous in the beginning of their relationship, it usually wasn't. It was planned. You made dates in advance, planned special treats, dressed carefully, and looked forward to being together. Planning sex does not diminish the fun and excitement of lovemaking. It adds to it. Contrary to popular opinion, making a decision in advance to have sex creates anticipation and can make sex just as exciting as when you were dating. In fact, it may be just the incentive you need to get the sparks flying again.

SCHEDULE SEX ON YOUR CALENDAR

In my classes, I devote several hours to teaching my students that scheduling sex is the best way to ensure that their relationship will be filled with intimacy and romance. Although the idea that scheduling sex will guarantee excitement is usually met with disbelief, once the students test the idea, they realize it's true.

Jack's attitude was typical of the scores of men in my classes who could not imagine recapturing the spontaneity they had shared with their mates before the kids came along. "Walking around nude, having sex anywhere or anytime, just isn't possible now that we have kids," he complained.

I told Jack the same thing I've told countless others. It's *not* impossible, if you and your mate are willing to sit down together and schedule time to be alone. The way I see it, you have two ways to arrange it. Either you and your mate can leave the house and go to a hotel, or your children can leave the house and stay with neighbors, friends, or relatives. In either case, you'll be free to walk around nude and, if you're in your own house, you can enjoy making love in any room of the house.

"You were right," Jack admitted one night in class.

"At first I thought it was ridiculous to schedule our lovemaking, but once we decided to do it, we really looked forward to our romantic evening alone. It sure beats the nothingness we were experiencing before."

Once you have scheduled sex on your calendar, try something different. Instead of hiring a sitter so you can dine out and go to a movie or the theater, why not get a sitter so you and your mate can enjoy an evening of sex in a hotel or motel? It will cost about the same amount of money, but it will be more fun, and you'll have a happy glow that lasts long after the evening ends.

Bonnie, the mother of three children, wrote to tell me how important the romantic rendezvous she and her husband have started taking are to her.

"We took your advice and once every three months we hire the baby-sitter to come on a Saturday, around 3 o'clock in the afternoon. I make the kids' dinner ahead of time so all the sitter has to do is serve it and clean up. My husband and I check into a nice hotel about 3:30 in the afternoon, where we enjoy an adult film on the VCR, make love, order room service and spend the rest of the evening talking and being close. We'll check out by midnight and we're home by 12:30 A.M.

"The best part is that just making the reservation creates lots of excited anticipation beforehand and the special feeling of closeness lingers long after the night ends."

Building anticipation is a technique that heightens the pleasure of a romantic evening as much as it heightens the pleasure of the actual act of sex. I've always advised my students to build anticipation into their plans to spend intimate time together.

A student who took my advice was Paulette, the

mother of two small children. "Now that we schedule sex on our calendar, we've started flirting again. I'll leave notes a few days before our date telling my husband how much I'm looking forward to our evening together. Or, we'll be watching TV with the kids and I'll write a number on his back or arm with my finger which tells him how many days we have left before our scheduled night. Sometimes he'll call me from work to tell me that he can't concentrate because he's thinking about me. Other times, he'll call and give me a detailed account of what he intends to do to me. It's so much fun," she said.

Giving your mate a small gift that relates to your scheduled time together is a great way to build anticipation and is one way to begin an intimate encounter before the actual event. The following are some of the items my students suggest, based on their own experience:

- A matchbook from the restaurant where you have reservations
- Scented body oil or lotion with the promise of a massage
- Bubble bath or bath salts with a note describing how and where you'll be lathering up
- Sexy lingerie for her, silk boxer shorts or brief bikinis for him, to add some visual stimulation
- A favorite X-rated video, gift-wrapped in paper and ribbon
- A love letter telling your mate how much you look forward to your time together
- A bottle of her favorite perfume or his favorite cologne
- A book of poetry or a love story to read together
- An erotic book

- A red rose every day for a week before your rendezvous
- A tape or CD of romantic music

BE SNEAKY AND LEARN ABOUT STEALING TIME

Everyone I talk to agrees that much of the excitement of their early sexual experiences was the result of having to sneak behind their parents' back. Likewise, a lot of the thrill of an affair is a result of sneaking away to a hotel during lunch, meeting in an out-of-the-way place after work, and stealing whatever time you can to be together. Now that you are parents, you can make a decision to be sneaky and steal time to be alone with each other, and you'll find that much of your initial excitement will return. The only difference is that now you'll be sneaking behind your children's backs, instead of your parents'.

There are many ways you can be sneaky and steal time together. Here are just a few:

- Set your alarm to go off an hour earlier in the morning, make love while the children are still asleep, and start your day a new and wonderful way.
- While the children are busy eating breakfast or watching cartoons, join your mate in the shower. Wash each other's hair and soap each other's bodies. The sensual memory will remain with you all day.
- When your children are young, their nap time can signal your opportunity to make love.
- When your children are older and involved with outside activities, the time they're away from the

house is the time for you and your mate to meet for an "afternoon delight."

• After the kids go off to school in the morning, you and your mate can decide to be late to work for a very important reason.

Sex doesn't always have to be orchestrated or anticipated to be good. I don't know how many of you had to sneak around to have sex before you were able to be open, but we've all heard stories about some of the ingenious ways our friends or acquaintances stole time together. You can bet that those stolen moments were usually what we would call a "quickie." As long as you can lock the door to ensure privacy, you can steal the few minutes you need for a quickie. I've heard stories of couples who got together in the garage when they went out to empty the trash. She leaned up against the wall and wrapped her legs around his waist as he supported her at the right height. The kids were upstairs working on homework and didn't miss their parents for the five or ten minutes they were otherwise engaged. Another couple I know of regularly have sex while they're in the basement doing the laundry. "In fact," jokes one woman, "I love doing it on the washer, during the spin cycle."

Susan, a student of mine who has been happily married for more than twenty-five years, has this to say about stealing time:

"My husband, Craig, was my best friend before the children came along, and I've always been careful to keep it that way. As much as I love my children, Craig is the one who stimulates my mind, as well as my body.

"Usually, I get the children ready for school while

my husband is getting ready for work. The kids leave on the school bus, and my husband kisses me good-bye and leaves for work.

"But sometimes, as Craig is getting into his car, I'll stand on the balcony outside our bedroom and shout his name. When he looks up, he sees me mouthing the words, 'Do You Wanna...?' and a huge smile appears on his face. Beaming, he asks, 'Really?' and I nod my head. He comes running up the stairs, and we make love. He has never once worried about getting to work late or letting a client wait. Lovemaking has always come first for both of us."

When Cathy, a teacher of "Light His Fire" in Ohio, was on a local radio talk show, the host made the following statement: "Once you have kids, you can forget about having spontaneous sex or sex outside the bedroom." Then he turned to Cathy and asked, "Do you agree with that?" Cathy responded, "Well, no, I don't. My husband just finished building a deck around our house. We have two children, and when they went to bed, we decided to 'break in' the new deck, if you know what I mean." A few days later Cathy called to tell me that after she made that comment, several men called in to say that they were going to the lumberyard immediately to buy some wood!

YOU CAN BECOME MORE SPONTANEOUS

As a general rule, children are very spontaneous. That's because they haven't yet learned to censor their constant flow of thoughts and ideas. Typically, they have a thought, decide it's a great idea, and a few seconds later they are acting on it. Spontaneity is how fast you can make a decision to act or not act on a thought you may have. The formula looks like this.

$$IDEA + DECISION + ACTION = SPONTANEITY$$

As we grow older, we learn to censor our thoughts, sift through our ideas, and delay our actions until it's an appropriate time to act. As a result, we lose much of our spontaneity. We can become more spontaneous by being open to our ideas, deciding quickly how and when to implement an idea, and then following through with an action. By practicing spontaneity, you will find that you will get good ideas more frequently, you will make spur-of-the-moment decisions more easily, and you will do more exciting things than you have ever done before. The following scenarios will help demonstrate the evolution of a spontaneous act.

Scenario 1: You are in a department store shopping for clothes for your children.

Idea:

As you pass by the lingerie department, you *think*, It's been so long since I bought a sexy nightgown.

Decision:

Instead of letting the thought go by without acting on it, stop and *decide* whether to buy yourself a nightie or not.

Action:

Act on your decision, by buying the negligee and wearing it that night instead of your usual sweats.

Scenario 2: You're at work at the end of a long day. You've been putting in lots of extra hours and effort the last few weeks, and you're really exhausted.

Idea:

You *think*, I know I've been neglecting my mate

lately. What we need is a little time away, just the two of us.

Decision:

Instead of leaving the office and going home, *decide* to take time to call some nearby hotels and see what kind of weekend packages they offer.

Action:

Act on your decision by calling the baby-sitter to see if she's available and booking the room. Send your mate a sexy note inviting him or her to meet you at the hotel on the appointed date.

Scenario 3: It's Saturday. You've just had a birthday party in the backyard for your five-year-old son. The yard is still filled with balloons.

Idea:

You *think*, Wouldn't it be great to make love out here tonight, instead of cleaning up this mess?

Decision:

Instead of popping the balloons and putting them in the trash, *decide* to suggest the idea to your mate.

Action:

Whisper in your mate's ear, "Let's have our own private party out here under the stars tonight. We've already decorated."

Before you know it, your mate will say, "Boy, are you becoming spontaneous. I never know what to expect anymore. You are the most exciting person to be with."

IT'S NOW OR NEVER

It may seem like a paradox, but becoming spontaneous takes a lot of practice. Most people get impulsive, romantic ideas at least occasionally, but instead of acting on them, they tend to think, "Not right now," or "This is not a good time" instead of "Right now," and "This is the perfect time." By acting on your thoughts, instead of censoring them, you will gradually develop the ability to be spontaneous.

We talked about this in the women's class one night, and I was amazed to hear how many women admitted that often during their busy day, even at the most inappropriate times, they thought about sex.

Arleen, a stockbroker and mother of two teenagers, said, "More than once I've been right in the middle of a client meeting, when the thought of having sex with my husband crosses my mind. Of course, I put the thought right out of my head because I can't just leave the client, can I?"

A woman named Charlotte said, "I'll be feeding the kids lunch and all of a sudden I'm really in the mood for sex, but it's the middle of the day, and I know Simon is busy at work. What am I supposed to do? Interrupt him?"

In both cases, my answer is yes. At least once in a while, stop what you are doing and make that phone call. Let your mate know you are feeling sexy and are thinking about the two of you making love. After all, why waste a sexy thought? *A sensual thought is wasted when it's not communicated.* Who knows, in the best-case scenario, he'll drop what he's doing and rush to be with you. The worst-case scenario is a mate who can't come home or meet you for a rendezvous, but who'll have a smile on his or her face for the rest of the day.

Many of the men who take "Light Her Fire" would like to be more spontaneous, and are eager to learn. They love this part of the class, because when we go through the formula they realize they have the power to do something about it. They learn that the longer they wait to act on a romantic idea, the stronger the possibility that something will change the feeling they originally had.

Ryan is a perfect example. Feeling very romantic as a result of the class, he stopped on his way home for a bottle of wine. He thought, When the time is right, I'll share this with Anne in front of the fireplace. Mentally, he began to plan this perfect evening. I'll wait until the kids are asleep, and while Anne takes her nightly bath I'll set up the family room with music, candlelight, and flowers, he dreamed. Maybe I'll even buy her a new nightie. That night he put the wine away in his closet for safekeeping. The next day his youngest child came down with the flu, and within days the other two followed. A week later, he had the flu, and a week after his bout, his wife had her turn. Over a month had gone by, and the bottle was aging nicely in the closet when he told the class this story.

Ryan said, "My mistake was *waiting* for the perfect night, instead of *making* it the perfect night when I first felt romantic. Instead of all the elaborate plans I had going on in my head, it would have been better to bring home the wine and just have a simple toast."

VARIETY IS THE SPICE OF LIFE

Couples with children are often so tied down with the routine and responsibility of raising a family that they become *working* partners instead of *loving* partners. Frequently, they become bored with their sex life because it's so predictable. They're in the habit of always making love at the same time, in the same way, and in the same place. Sometimes, this boredom leads one

of the partners to have an affair, but the key to a more
exciting sex life is not to change your *partner*, but to
change the *place*. The easiest way to get out of a "bed
room rut" is to get out of the bedroom. Do something
different. Break away from the familiar. That ordinary
room in your home can become the setting for an ex-
traordinary experience that will keep you smiling for
quite some time. Be more like the comedian who was
asked if he thought sex was dirty. "Only when it's
good," he replied.

Remember when you and your mate first set up
housekeeping together? Your imaginations probably
worked overtime as you thought up new ways to
christen each room of the house. I'm sure that you
even surprised yourselves at the "wild and wicked"
thoughts you had. Dirty, naughty, wild, and sneaky
sex are all too often lost when lovers become parents.
The fear that our children might walk in on us having
spontaneous sex is one reason why we may confine
our lovemaking to the bedroom. Of course, you
should pick times when you're fairly certain that your
children are not likely to catch you "in the act," but
sometimes accidents do happen. If your child should
happen to walk in on you while you are making love,
don't panic. Try to keep your sense of humor and
treat the interruption in a calm manner. If you over-
react, you may scare your child and give him a negative message about lovemaking.

You can recapture that feeling of daring and forbid-
den sex if you'll let your imagination run wild, as so
many of my graduates have. You too can use:

• The table in your kitchen or dining room for more
  than just paying the bills or serving meals
• The countertop for more than just chopping vege-

tables. (Who can forget the movie *Fatal Attraction*?)
- The couch in the den for more than just watching TV
- The living room floor for more than just gathering dust
- The top of the washer or dryer for more than just cleaning clothes
- The bathtub or shower for more than just bathing
- The backseat of your car for more than just hauling groceries

I'll never forget Howard, a man in his forties who had been married for more than twenty years, when he came to class very excited one evening. He told us that while he was driving home from last week's class, he was listening to fifties music on the radio, and it reminded him of the time when he and his wife were dating. "Since we were only teenagers when we fell in love, the only privacy we could find was my car," Howard said. "When I got home from class, I asked my wife to follow me out to the garage where I gave her a long, passionate kiss. Then I opened the car door. When my wife giggled and asked, 'What do you think you're doing?' I told her, 'Reliving our teenage years.'" Howard said they had more fun than they've had in years—"And do you know it was the first time in all our married life that we began sex with our clothes on?" he added with a grin.

BE UNPREDICTABLE

There's nothing more boring than knowing a person so well that you can predict his every move. If you're guilty of the crime of predictability, you can escape a life sentence of boredom with a little creativity. It's not necessary to have an elaborate plan in order to surprise your mate. Creating a sense of mystery every so often is really very simple. All you have to do is something completely out of character occasionally so that your partner says, "Boy, I never know what to expect with you. You really surprise me." Doing something unexpected and unpredictable is guaranteed to make your heart beat faster and put butterflies in your stomach, as well as your mate's.

One reader wrote to tell me how she finally mustered enough courage to surprise her husband. "I am thirty-five years old and have four children ranging in age from five to thirteen years. I also work part time as an image consultant," Cindy wrote.

"My husband's fortieth birthday was approaching and when I mentioned to a friend that I didn't know what to get him as a gift she gave me a copy of *Light His Fire*. I really got motivated and instead of my usual shirt and tie gift, I was determined to 'knock his socks off' as you put it. I arranged to have the same friend who gave me the book baby-sit. On the day of his birthday, I called my husband at work and told him to come to room #431 of a nearby hotel at exactly 7:00 P.M. I arrived at the hotel early and covered the ceiling of the room with balloons and put a bottle of champagne in the ice bucket. When my husband arrived, I was waiting on the bed wearing just a pair of high heels and ribbons in every color you could think of. I had bows around my neck, streamers around my thighs, silk cords around my ankles. I told my husband that every time he took a sip of champagne he'd get to untie one ribbon.

"My husband couldn't believe his eyes. He commented that he thought he knew me so well that he would have bet a million dollars that I wasn't capable of doing something like this. Well, I certainly shocked him, and myself to be quite honest. It's fun doing something different. No more shirts and ties for my husband."

While Cindy's story is extravagant, there are lots of simple things you can do to surprise your mate. For instance, take a look at what you usually wear to bed. Even though you have children, you can exchange that warm flannel nightgown or those cool summer pajamas for a sexy surprise. He can exchange his boring pajamas or Jockey shorts for a pair of silk boxer shorts, a handsome smoking jacket, or sexy colored bikinis. If you and your mate were having an affair and meeting for a secret rendezvous, what would you wear? Certainly not what you wear to bed night after night. Both of you should go on a shopping spree for special garments that are "for your eyes only."

Hannah said this really hit home for her. "After you talked about this in class, I took a good, hard look at myself," she revealed. "I used to have a few really sexy outfits that Brad just loved, but somehow they got replaced by much more 'suitable' attire for the mother of two little boys.

"One evening, I was looking at a department-store catalog. I pointed to a pretty nightgown on the lingerie page and asked Brad how he liked it. He pointed to the opposite page, where a model wore a plunging black bra, skimpy panties, and a garter belt, and said, 'I like this one a lot more.' I just rolled my eyes and dismissed his opinion. But later I started thinking about how I'd lost my sexuality since the boys came along.

"The next day I made my big purchase. That night, after the boys went to sleep, I took a long bubble bath and came to bed dressed in the very outfit Brad had pointed to in the catalog. He was so surprised. He kept telling me over and over how sexy I looked. And, you know, I felt sexy again for the first time in a long time."

Mind you, I'm not talking about trying to surprise your mate every day. But if you were to wear what you normally wear to bed most of the time, and then once a week or so wear a surprise, it would be terrific. For example, you could wear:

- Pajama tops and no bottom
- Pajama bottoms and no top
- No top and no bottom

Do what you normally do most of the time, and then, every once in a while, do something different. For instance, if you always get up on the left side of the bed, crawl over your mate and get up on the other side tomorrow. When your mate asks, "Hey, what are you doing?" just say, "I wanted to start the day a little different, so I thought I'd get up on the right side. Besides, now I can kiss you."

If you always make love after the evening news, set the alarm for an hour earlier and make love in the morning. Surprise your mate by joining him or her in the shower. The idea is to do something that is a little bit different than what your mate is used to. It isn't necessary to buy an expensive gift, or do something extravagant, to surprise your mate. In fact, simpler is often better. The following are just a few ways to put the element of surprise into your relationship:

- Give your mate a lingering kiss when he or she least expects it.

- Attach a note to the morning newspaper that says, "News Flash. I Love You."
- At mealtime, nibble on your mate's ear as you pass by and say "Umm. You taste good, too."
- The next time you're at a restaurant, sit opposite your mate. Instead of letting "your fingers do the walking," let your feet do some sexy "walking."
- Arrive home from work with something in your hand besides the keys.
- Greet your mate at the front door wearing something sexy and provocative.

ADULT ENCOUNTERS OF THE SEXY KIND

Over the years, I've collected many stories from couples who don't let anything or anyone get in the way of their special memories. If you once knew the joy of romance, but your imagination and memory have become a little rusty from lack of use, these ideas may help you.

1. Love Slave

Many couples have learned that acting out a fantasy is a great way to keep romance and sexuality alive in their relationship. Dory and Brad take turns pretending they are love slaves. "When it's my turn to be the love slave," Dory writes, "my husband is allowed to ask me for any favor he wants. I must fulfill his fantasy, which usually has to do with making love. Then, when it's my turn, I can ask him to do anything I want. This is when I can get him to go shopping with me for a new outfit or cuddle in bed for the whole evening. For us it's the perfect solution. He gets his sexual fulfillment, and I get the attention and affection I want."

2. *Massage Parlor*

A couple in the Midwest purchased a massage table that can be folded and put under the bed when it's not in use. "We take turns being the customer," they write. The "customer" lies nude on the massage table, covered by a sheet. The "masseuse" enters the room completely naked and is obligated to do anything the customer wants. "My husband's massage usually ends with us having sex," writes the wife, "but I prefer to have a nice, long massage and end up falling asleep in each other's arms."

3. *Strangers*

Some couples like to pretend they are strangers. There are many different scenarios to play out, but one man from Chicago writes, "My wife and I are active in a lot of organizations and we have to attend many functions. To make things interesting, sometimes we pretend that we are strangers meeting for the first time. We begin flirting with each other, talk, touch and wind up going home with each other. It's amazing how this simple game helps make a boring social function fun. An added bonus is that seeing each other as strangers makes us remember why we fell in love in the first place."

4. *Strip Monopoly*

Here is a new twist on an old game. Earl writes, "We'll play regular Monopoly with the kids, but then Marie and I have our own version when the kids go to sleep. Instead of paying rent when we land on the other one's property, we remove an article of clothing. Just in case the game lasts too long, the first one to PASS GO ten times, collects!"

5. *Private Bet*

One reader wrote to tell me that although she once hated sports, she's now an enthusiastic viewer. "My husband watches sports on T.V. every weekend. I really resented it until I decided to make his interest in sports work *for* us instead of *against* us. We each bet on which team we think is going to win and by how many points. The person who loses has to do whatever the winner wants. Just last week, I lost and had to serve my husband dinner completely nude. Of course, I shipped the kids off to Grandma's house. We had so much fun that the next time I win, I'm going to have him do the same thing. Now I can't wait to see who's playing on T.V. so I can wind up playing with my husband."

6. *Whipped-Cream Delight*

How about this for an idea? "Years ago," writes a woman in Boulder, "my husband and I discovered the pleasure of using ready-to-serve whipped topping to make sex more interesting. Kissing different parts of the body is simply delicious when they've been topped with whipped cream. We have nicknamed this activity *dessert*. We often will talk about dessert right in front of the children because it goes right over their heads. At breakfast, I'll say, 'Gee, I have a new dessert in mind for tonight' and John knows exactly what I'm talking about. He'll get a huge smile and say, 'I can't wait.' Then the real fun begins.

"He'll call me during the day and say something like, 'Did you get all the ingredients for your new dessert?' I get a lot of pleasure knowing that work isn't the only thing on his mind. Sometimes, I'll call him and tell him to stop by the store and pick up something for dessert. On several occasions he's bought the topping secretly and put it in the refrigerator. When I discover it the next morning I always call to let him know and we both look forward to dessert that evening. This private game between us has kept a special spark in our marriage."

7. *For Your Eyes Only*

This idea comes from Tampa. Grace writes, "To celebrate each new season, my husband and I like to spend a night in a hotel room while my mother watches our three children. Before our prearranged evening, I send him an invitation to view the new line of (summer, fall, winter, or spring) lingerie. I go shopping and buy several pieces of sexy lingerie, such as teddies, lacy garter belts, net stockings, negligees, and even crotchless panties. At the hotel, I put on a private fashion show for him. I select music that will make me feel sexy, have chilled champagne, and order appetizers sent to the room. I give my husband a pencil and paper and he judges the garments, selecting the one he likes best. Later, at a time when he least expects it, I send his favorite garment to his office with a note that says:

Roses are red, violets are blue.
Bring this tonight and I'll wear it for you.

8. *Dirty Dancing*

For Dwayne in Long Island, the fun begins when his two children are asleep. "We'll put on our favorite music, take off all our clothes and dance nude in the privacy of our bedroom. We both love the feeling of our bodies touching, while we dance cheek to cheek. Whenever I buy a new tape, I send it to my wife at the office and she knows it's time to *dance*.

9. A Love Trail

This idea comes from San Diego. Hilary writes, "I love flowers. To me, flowers spell r-o-m-a-n-c-e. So, when I'm in the mood for love, I'll leave a trail of flowers from the front door to our bedroom. I place a vase of water on our night stand beside the bed. When my husband comes home and sees the flowers he knows that our daughter is at our neighbor's house and dinner will be *very late.* He picks up each flower and when he's collected all of them, puts them in the vase beside the bed. Then we spend the evening making love, tantalized by the scent of my favorite flowers. Imagine my surprise one Saturday when I came home from shopping and found roses leading to the bedroom. My husband sure knows the way to my heart!"

10. Getting Your Money's Worth

I met a young couple on a cruise recently who told me they've been married ten years and have two girls, ages five and eight. Every year they celebrate their anniversary by going to a hotel. "We check in the night of our anniversary and have a wonderful evening," they said. "The next morning, we ask for a late checkout, which is usually two P.M. We both go to work that morning and then meet in our room again at noon for a quick and exciting midday rendezvous. This way, we really feel we're getting our money's worth."

11. Seduce Me, Baby

Randall, from Colorado Springs, writes, "I came to the realization a few years ago that my wife and I hardly ever felt the urge for sex at the same time. If she was in the mood, I was too tired. If I was in the mood, she had a headache. When we finally sat down one night and really talked about it, we came up with a great idea. We decided that if one of us was in the mood for sex, it was up to that person to get the other one in the mood. That was, after all, how it worked before the kids came along. We used to spend a lot of time seducing each other, but we had just gotten lazy. I was the one who suggested we call our game 'Seduce Me, Baby.'

"We agreed that there was no obligation on the other person's part to give in. The first time I wanted to seduce my wife, I decided to take her to a movie. In the middle of the show I started touching her seductively and we began some very passionate kissing. Before you knew it, we were into heavy petting. We both got so turned on that we left before the end of the movie, and we still don't know how it ended.

"On another occasion, my wife came to my office in the middle of the day and locked my door. The rest is too X-rated to tell. This has really worked for us and we happily spend a lot of time thinking about how to seduce each other."

FIFTY-ONE WAYS TO LIGHT A FIRE

The following list, "Fifty-one Ways to Keep the Fire Lit When the Kids Are Driving You Crazy," can be used for added inspiration when you feel as though there is nothing more to life than diapers, two o'clock feedings, potty training, baby talk, soccer, Little League, and car pools. These are suggestions only. There are no rules to follow, no order in which you must do them, and it doesn't matter which one of you initiates the action. It's the message that matters—not the method. A man (or woman) who is willing to take time from his busy life to make his mate feel special sends a powerful message of love that says, "I didn't do this for our children, our friends, our relatives, or my co-workers. I did this just for you. I want to spend time with you alone to show you how special you are and how complete you make my life."

Please don't be concerned about doing it "right." There is no right way. Only your way—from the heart. Customize any of these ideas to fit your own personality.

FIFTY-ONE WAYS TO KEEP THE FIRE LIT WHEN THE KIDS ARE DRIVING YOU CRAZY

1. *Have I Got News for You*
   Get up a little earlier and get the newspaper before your mate does. Attach a note to the section you know he or she always reads. For example:
   World News: "You're the world's greatest lover."
   Comics: "You're my funny valentine."
   Sports Page: "I want to score some points with you tonight," or "Let's wrestle tonight."
   Classifieds: "Wanted—You in my arms tonight."
   Food: "Nothing is as delicious and tantalizing as you."
   Business: "Let's get down to some serious business tonight."
   Real Estate: "Let's play house tonight."
2. *Make It Difficult to Concentrate*
   If your mate is all work and no play, this is a guaranteed distraction. Send a pair of silk boxer

shorts to his office (now available in washable silk called "Naked Silk") or send a sexy teddy to her office. Use a padded manila envelope marked PERSONAL AND CONFIDENTIAL. Put some heart stickers on the envelope, so no one else dares open it. Enclose a note for her that says, "Roses are red, violets are blue. I'd sure like to see this teddy on you." For him, enclose a note that says, "Roses are red, violets are blue. I'd sure like to see these silk shorts on you."

3. *The Second Time Around*

I believe that not only should a couple celebrate their wedding anniversary each year, but they should also celebrate the date they met or had their first date. If you're not already doing so, start this ritual now. Every year, on the anniversary of your first date, celebrate by recreating the same situation. Go to the same restaurant. If you were out with friends, invite the same people to help you celebrate. Include as much detail as you can, but this time try a different ending. Reserve the honeymoon suite at the hotel of your choice, where you will spend the night. Be sure to toast that special day. After all, if you hadn't met or gone out that first time, there would be no anniversary.

4. *Toys R U*

The couple that plays together stays together. Take a trip to the local toy store and let the little boy or girl inside you come out to play. This time, instead of buying toys for your children, you and your mate can have a lot of fun buying toys for yourselves. You could buy:

• A rubber duck

Play with your duck in the bathtub or spa.

- Boats or submarines
  Float one in a lake or stream.
- Bubbles
  See who can blow the most bubbles.
- Water pistols
  Have a duel with the new supersized water guns.
- Bubble gum
  See who can blow the biggest bubbles.
- Kites
  Be flighty and fly kites on a windy day.
- Model plane or car
  Build and paint a classic car or vintage plane together.
- Hula-Hoops
  Put on some music and see who can keep the hoop spinning the longest.
- Jigsaw puzzle
  Relax in the evening with a puzzle of at least five hundred pieces. Use puzzle glue to keep it together, and hang it on the wall as a reminder of the time you spent together.
- Roller blades
  Keep fit this fun new way.
- Coloring book and crayons
  Have a contest and let the children be the judges. Categories can include Prettiest, Most Colorful, and Funniest.

  Whatever you do, don't let the kids get your toys!

5. Let the Maid Do It

One day, when you know that you and your mate are going to spend the day cleaning house, surprise your mate by hiring a cleaning service instead. When the cleaning crew shows up, give your mate a note that says:

Cleaning up is hard to do
A picnic would be more fun for you.
I'll bring the blanket, wine and cheese
All you must do is get ready, *please*.

Make arrangements in advance for the children to be taken care of, and have everything ready for a private picnic together. Give your mate time to recover from the shock and change into something comfortable, and then enjoy a beautiful day together in a secluded spot.

6. *The Body Beautiful*

In the sixties, body painting was in vogue, and it can still be a fun activity for you and your mate. Find a costume shop or art store that sells body paint, and decorate each other's naked bodies.

7. *Laughter Is the Best Medicine*

Spend a day laughing together. Share a joke book, rent a funny movie, or go to a comedy club.

8. *Love Trail*

When you'd like to lead your mate down a path to making love, leave a trail that begins at the front door and ends at the bed—where you are waiting. You can leave a trail of:

- Flowers
- Colored string
- Candles
- Articles of your clothing
- Arrows made out of craft paper
- Candy kisses

9. Stand-up Romance

Dancing is probably the first socially acceptable form of romantic touching that you experienced. Remember when you and your mate used to dance so close together that it would have been impossible to slide a plastic credit card between your bodies? Relive those years. Get a recording of the songs that were popular when you were dating and spend an evening rediscovering the erotic pleasure of stand-up romance.

10. Home Sweet Home

This is a wonderful way to allow your imagination to run wild. Pick a few of the most expensive developments in your area and visit the model homes. Once inside your dream house, pretend it is yours. Imagine that you've given all the servants the day off, and you are all alone. Greet your mate at the front door with a passionate kiss. Steal more kisses in each room. This fantasy will probably be most satisfactory if undertaken on a day that is un-crowded. If you go on a weekend, there will be too many people joining you on your tour. On the other hand, if someone does catch you kissing, they'll just be envious of your obvious passion for each other.

11. Shopping Spree

This involves an entire day and evening, so make sure you hire a capable sitter for your children. It can also be very expensive, but if money is not a consideration, it can be a wonderful adventure. Invite your mate to go to dinner at a very elegant restaurant. When he or she voices the usual "But I don't have a thing to wear," just say, "No problem." Spend the day shopping for new outfits for both of you.

For Him	For Her
Underwear	Undergarments
Suit, or jacket and pants	Stockings
Shirt	Dress
Tie	Shoes
Socks	Accessories
Belt	Trip to makeup counter for free makeup demonstration

Be sure to remove the tags and wear your new clothes right out of the store. Then go straight to dinner feeling and looking like a "million dollars." I guarantee that you'll have a wonderful "dessert" that night.

12. *Going Up?*

Choose a hotel that has a nice restaurant or coffee shop and make a reservation there for one night without telling your mate. Then, on the evening of the reservation, suggest that the two of you go to that hotel's restaurant. After dinner, suggest a romantic ride in the elevator. As you kiss your mate, push the appropriate floor. When the elevator stops, take your mate's hand and playfully lead him or her to the room you have reserved.

13. *Wear Your Birthday Suit*

Go skinny-dipping when the rest of the world is asleep. One couple wrote to tell me that not only did they go skinny-dipping at a private beach a half hour from their house, but they both rode back in the car completely nude.

14. *Bind Your Love*

This is a repeat from my book *Light His Fire,* but it

was so popular that I had to include it here. Use silk scarves to tie his hands and feet (loosely) to the bedposts. Use a chair if your bed isn't properly equipped. Tease him a long time before making love to him. Men wrote to tell me they just love the idea of being completely passive for a change, and women wrote to tell me that they've used ribbon, rope, pantyhose, bras, and other interesting items as restraints. At one lecture I gave, a woman in her seventies came up to me at the break and said, "Honey, Ace bandages work just great!"

15. *Write the "Book of Love"*
Write your own personal love story. Begin with how you met and include what you did on your first date and how you felt. Continue describing your life together. Talk about the birth of your children and any other major events. When you complete it, have your story printed and bound. It will be a wonderful gift that can be handed down from generation to generation.

16. *Destination Anywhere*
Set aside a day with absolutely no agenda except to spend it together without the children. Get in the car and start driving with no destination in mind. As the saying goes, "Any road will take you there, if you don't know where you're going." Stop whenever you feel like it. Eat whenever you are hungry. Explore a new neighborhood or take some of those interesting side roads you've always wondered about. This is a great adventure for people who always have to plan ahead. Let go for one day and see how free you feel. You'll know where you were going when you get there.

17. *Treasure Hunt*
Have a jeweler cut a gold coin in half and mount

each half on a gold chain. Place the necklaces in a
jewelry box with a note that says, "Without you,
I'm incomplete," or "To my better half," and pick
a spot to bury your treasure. On parchment paper
draw a series of pirate maps with progressive directions to the buried treasure. Each map should
have directions to the next map. Hide each map in
a different location, and on the last map use a large
"X" to mark the spot where the treasure is buried.
Give your mate the first map and send him on a
treasure hunt. When your mate finds the treasure,
fasten the chains around each other's necks and de-
clare your love for each other.

18. *One Is Not Enough*

For a truly special evening, go to a different restaurant for each part of your meal. Explain to your
mate that no one restaurant is good enough for him
or her. Start at a restaurant that has great appetizers. Next, go to one that is known for its outstanding salad bar. After your salad, go to a restaurant
that has fabulous entrées. End the meal at a place
that is known for its mouth-watering desserts. If
you really want to go all out, have the waiter at
each restaurant present a gift to your love such as
a rose, perfume, or cologne, a Mylar balloon that
says, "I Love You," a card, or a stuffed animal.

19. *A Love for All Seasons*

You don't have to wait for a special holiday to have
a celebration. You can usher in each new season
with a toast to your health and happiness and by
making love in a place that is unique to that time
of year. For example:

• In summer, make love . . .
  On the beach

In the ocean
At a lake
In a swimming pool
• In winter, make love . . .
In a mountain cabin
In front of the fireplace
In a hot tub
• In the fall, make love . . .
On a pile of leaves
In a hayloft
On a hayride
• In the spring, make love . . .
In a meadow
On a grassy hill
In a green pasture

20. *Adrift on a Sea of Love*

Take your mate on a romantic boat ride. Rent a boat and bring along a portable stereo to provide romantic music; a bottle of wine, champagne, or apple cider to quench your thirst; and finger foods to curb your appetite. Depending on your budget, you can rent a rowboat, gondola, canoe, sailboat, motorboat, or yacht. Although the size of the boat may vary, the romantic feelings will be exactly the same.

21. *Rekindle the Flames of Passion*

There is nothing as warm and cozy as a crackling campfire. The flames have a hypnotic effect that seems to relax us and invite intimate conversation. Most people only sit around a campfire when there is a large gathering. This time, build a campfire for just the two of you. Plan a trip to the beach, the woods, a lake, or some other outdoor location where you can build a fire. Pack up some dry

wood, matches, newspaper, blankets, and a couple
of lawn chairs. Bring along some wire hangers for
toasting marshmallows and a thermos of hot chocolate. (For a delectable treat, try a mixture of hot
chocolate, coffee, and Kahlúa liqueur.)

22. *Find the Hidden Message*
Use a highlighter pen to create a hidden message
in a magazine your mate enjoys reading. Start at
the front and highlight appropriate words on suc-
ceeding pages. Leave a note at the beginning of the
magazine, letting your mate know that if he or she
copies down each highlighted word, the end result
will be a message from your heart.

23. *Find Romance in the Yellow Pages*
This adventure should be planned for a weekend
when your children can be away. Put the Yellow
Pages telephone directory in a place your mate is
sure to see it as soon as he or she wakes up. Write
a note on a romantic card explaining that you've
hidden little gifts all through the house and tape
the card to the front of the directory. Your mate's
job is to follow the instructions you've left in the
directory to find the gifts and eventually get to the
"grand prize." Using my own phone book as an
example, this is how it works:

- On the cover of the directory is a Post-it note
  that says, "Go to page 544." On page 544 a florist is highlighted, and another Post-it note says,
  "Go to the bathroom." In the tub, there is a single rose and another note.
- The second note says, "Turn to page 715 of the
  phone book." On that page a liquor store is
  highlighted, and a note says, "Look in the re-

frigerator." In the refrigerator, there is a chilled bottle of wine, and another note.

- This note says, "Turn to page 583." On page 583, a glass company is highlighted, and a message sends your mate to the kitchen cabinet. In the cabinet are two beautiful wineglasses with ribbon tied around them and a fourth note.
- The fourth note says, "Go to page 1161," where closet organizers are advertised. One of the ads is highlighted, and another note says, "Go look in our closet." In the closet is a suitcase for your mate, packed for an overnight trip. On the suitcase is a fifth note.
- This note says, "Go to page 626." On that page, a particular hotel has been highlighted, and a last note says, "Meet me in the lobby at three o'clock this afternoon."

A lot of work, yes. But once it's done, you'll be talking about it for years.

24. *Amuse Yourselves*

Leave the kids home and go to an amusement park, carnival, or county fair together. Hold hands, eat cotton candy, go on the merry-go-round, and try to win a stuffed animal. If you're not worrying about your kids having a good time, the kid in you can come out and play.

25. *While the Kids Are Away, the Folks Will Play*

Instead of hiring a baby-sitter to watch the children while you go out, have the baby-sitter take the kids to a double feature and you stay home. That should give you about three hours of uninterrupted time for romance. Don't you dare do any chores with this precious time!

26. *Rise and Shine*

This is a wonderful idea if you are too exhausted at night to be romantic. Set the dining-room table with a linen tablecloth and your best dinnerware and have a candlelight breakfast. You'll be amazed at how great eggs can taste when they're eaten in a romantic setting.

27. *Change Gears*

A change of scenery is good for the soul and stimulates the senses. If you live in the country, drive into the city and spend the day. If you live in the city, drive to the country and spend the day. If you live in the mountains, drive to the beach. If you live near the coast, drive to the mountains.

28. *Get "High" on Chocolate*

It's been said that chocolate is an aphrodisiac, producing the same "high" that one gets from falling in love. Whether it's true or not, one thing is for sure. Chocolate is always a welcome gift, especially when accompanied by a love note, such as "Sweets for my sweetheart," or "I'm sweet on you." Here are a few of my favorite chocolate gifts:

- Long-stemmed chocolate-chip cookies
- Long-stemmed chocolate roses
- Hershey's Kisses
- Godiva chocolates of any kind
- Chocolate Santa, Easter Bunny, heart
- Chocolate bars (Snickers, Almond Joy, Mounds, Milky Way, M&M's)

29. *Heating Up*

Get a book of matches from a dark, out-of-the-way restaurant. Send the matches to your mate at work with a note: "I'm hot for you. Meet me at this restaurant tonight at seven o'clock."

30. A Season of Fun

Buying season tickets to the theater, symphony, ball game, or concert is less expensive in the long run and guarantees good seats. The best part is that you are now committed to go out on a date regularly.

31. Dial-a-Ride

Although somewhat expensive, renting a limousine for an evening can be a very romantic affair. If your budget is limited, you could rent the limo and make your destination a quiet, secluded spot with a view. The ocean, a lake, or a river are a few ideas. If you live in the city, a bluff with a view of the city lights would be lovely. Listen to romantic music, drink a champagne toast to your love, and share some secrets.

32. Break Away to a Bed & Breakfast

For a truly romantic getaway, try a bed & breakfast instead of a hotel. B&Bs offer a taste of a lifestyle that eludes most of us. Often located in glorious settings, they are managed and decorated to make you feel like a pampered guest of the Rockefellers. There is nothing so romantic as a Victorian inn, complete with featherbeds, down comforters, lacy coverlets, and a room full of roses. While most hotel rooms look the same, every bed & breakfast offers a unique setting and ambiance designed to arouse all of your senses.

33. Dine in Elegance

Instead of spending the money on an expensive restaurant, why not plan a formal dinner for two at home? Set the table with your finest china and linens, place candles everywhere, and dress in your most elegant clothes. To add to the flavor of the evening, hire a maid to serve the meal and clean

up the kitchen, while the two of you retire to your
private quarters for a nightcap.

34. A Halloween Treat

Here's a fun way to celebrate Halloween. Each of
you rent a costume of a famous romantic couple
from history, and then play the role of that couple
throughout the evening. King Arthur and Guine-
vere, Romeo and Juliet, Cleopatra and Mark An-
tony, and Adonis and Aphrodite are just some
examples of whom you could dress up as. End the
evening by taking a bath together and bobbing for
apples in your bathtub.

35. A State of Bliss

Next Valentine's Day buy eight romantic cards.
Address each one to your mate and affix a "love"
stamp. Next, put each card inside another envelope, address it to the postmaster in each of the
following towns, and enclose a note asking that
your valentine be hand-stamped and mailed. Imagine your mate's surprise when he or she receives
your valentine sent from:

- Bliss, NY 14024
- Bridal Veil, OR 97010
- Kissimmee, FL 32741
- Loveland, CO 80537
- Loving, NM 88256
- Romance, WV 25175
- Valentine, TX 79854
- Valentine, NB 69201

An extra-special touch is to have all eight hand-
canceled envelopes mounted and framed.

36. Bedtime Stories

Take turns reading a book to each other just before you go to sleep. It's a wonderful way to end a day, snuggled in each other's arms.

37. A Heavenly Body

You can actually name a star after your mate. You can use your mate's proper name, but using a pet name might be more fun. Your mate will receive an embossed certificate, two star-spangled charts showing you where his star is located in the galaxy, and a booklet on the stars. The name will be registered in the International Star Registry's Swiss vault, and the names are written in the book called *Your Place in the Cosmos*. Send for an application to:

International Star Registry
1821 Willow Road
Northfield, IL 60093

38. Just a Jingle

Sometimes you're just too busy to take time for a long call to your mate, but one ring will let her know you are thinking of her. If your mate has a beeper, devise a secret code that means "I'm thinking of you."

39. A Romantic Workout

Take a dance class together. You can learn square dancing, ballroom dancing, folk dancing, or country-western dancing. Besides being great exercise, dancing keeps you laughing, loving, and healthy, and the night out together will energize you for the rest of the week.

40. Dinner in Bed

Feed the kids and then put the Do Not Disturb sign on your door. Order takeout Chinese food or pizza for yourselves, rent one of these wonderful romantic movies, and have dinner in bed while you watch:

Gone With the Wind
An Officer and a Gentleman
Romeo and Juliet
Funny Girl
Casablanca
When Harry Met Sally
Somewhere in Time
Pretty Woman

41. Rx for Love

Put your own label on an empty prescription bottle. On the label, type in your mate's name and the following prescription: *Take one as needed.* Fill the bottle with notes that have been crunched up into little pill-sized balls. Examples:

- A long, passionate kiss
- A romantic walk in the park holding hands
- An hour of necking in the backseat of the car
- A one-hour massage
- A romantic candlelight dinner

42. A Tape Made to Order

Record a cassette tape of romantic songs that are meaningful to the two of you and give it to your mate. Every time the tape is played, you'll be thought of.

43. Take Up a Collection

Every time you make love, put a dollar in a special jar. At the end of the year, use the money for a romantic treat.

44. Pamper Yourselves

Once in a while, everybody deserves a day just for themselves. Each of you select a day to be devoted solely to pampering yourself and catch up on all the luxuries you enjoyed before the kids came along.

FOR HER—Bubble bath, massage, makeover, hairstyling, manicure, pedicure, facial, lunch with the girls, curling up in bed with a good book, breakfast in bed, dinner out.

FOR HIM—Bubble bath, massage, haircut, manicure, pedicure, facial, watching sports on TV, an outing with the guys (golf, football game), breakfast in bed, favorite meal served to him in his easy chair.

45. Save It for a Rainy Day

Buy recordings of "Raindrops Keep Falling on My Head" and "Singing in the Rain" and put them away. Then, on the next rainy night, have an indoor picnic. Pack a picnic basket with a red-and-white-checkered tablecloth, grapes to hand-feed your mate, and an assortment of sandwiches. Spread your picnic in front of the fireplace and turn on the music. If you don't have a fireplace, the floor in any room will do just as long as you can cuddle, kiss, and enjoy looking out at the rain.

46. Car Theft

While your mate is at work, take the extra set of car keys and steal the car. Have it detailed or take it to a car wash and have it cleaned inside and out. When you return the car to its parking place, put a gift-wrapped cassette tape or CD on the passenger seat with a love note and instructions to listen to the new tape you bought (or made). This would be the perfect time to unveil your customized tape. Flowers on the driver's seat will complete your mission.

47. Joint Project

Undertake a project that the two of you can enjoy together—anything that provides you with a sense of purpose and togetherness. Although you may be working on a serious project, don't forget to have fun. Here are some suggestions:

- Buy an antique at a garage sale and refinish together.
- Redecorate a room together.
- Plant a flower box or vegetable garden.

48. Risky Business

Dare to be bold and take a risk. Any one of these exhilarating adventures can get that heart pumping and the adrenaline flowing. After all, you don't want to look back on your life and realize that you never took any chances, never did anything out of the ordinary.

- River rafting
- Skydiving
- Gliding
- Hang gliding
- Parasailing
- Jet skiing
- Rock climbing
- Snow skiing
- Hot-air ballooning

Make sure you get a video of your adventure. You'll be so proud, you'll want everyone you know to see it.

49. A Romantic Carriage Ride

The next time you're in a city that has one, plan to take a horse-drawn carriage ride. Take a blanket and some hot chocolate. Snuggle close and see the city through the eyes of two lovers.

50. Be a Star for a Day

Pretend you are fashion models. Hire a professional photographer and go on a fashion shoot. Each of you pack a variety of clothing from casual to formal, then seek out locations appropriate for each style of clothing. Wear tennis clothes and go to the tennis courts; go to the harbor and pose in front of a sailboat wearing boating attire; dress in suits and shoot at an office building; wear your formal clothes (rent a tuxedo, if necessary) and go to a luxurious hotel. Complete the fantasy by having dinner there and spending the night.

51. A Romantic Board Game for Two

A nice complement to any of the above ideas is a wonderful game that I have been recommending for years called *An Enchanting Evening*. It's love, laughter, and romance in a box. Each player writes down a secret wish that can be shared with his or her partner. The players move around the board and pick cards that encourage positive supportive responses and gentle sensual touching. The winner gets his or her wish fulfilled, but both players really win. *An Enchanting Evening* can be purchased by calling 1-800-776-7662. If you mention this book when you call, you will receive a 10% discount off the purchase price.

LHF Enterprises
P.O. Box 1511
Lake Forest, CA 92630

There you have it: fifty-one ways for parents to stay lovers; fifty-one ways to keep the sparks flying. This list was compiled from suggestions made by couples with children—couples who are still very much in love with each other. If you're serious about keeping the fire lit while raising your children, pick one of these ideas and begin planning today. Don't put it off for some future time. Remember, "A journey of a thousand miles begins with the first step."

ASSIGNMENT #5

Becoming a Better Parent

1. Explain to your children that parents need special time to be alone together, so that they can focus on each other and make each other feel good. If you have more than one child, your children will understand the need to focus on one person at a time, because they also crave that kind of special time.
2. In order to avoid unpleasant surprises while your children are learning to respect your mate's and your time alone together, hold some practice sessions. These can be times when you steal time together just to watch TV, talk, or read in the sanctuary of your bedroom. This way, when you want to make love in the future, you will know that the children are totally comfortable with what's expected of them.
3. Becoming more spontaneous can also be a tool for improving your relationship with your children. Instead of waiting until Christmas or a birthday to buy the children a gift, sometimes, when you see something you think they would particularly like, get it for them.

4. Do something unexpected for your children this week. You could tape a note in their lunch boxes, telling them you love them. You might arrange a special outing for your children and a friend, or you could surprise them by dropping by their school and taking them to lunch at their favorite fast-food restaurant.

Becoming a Better Partner

1. Buy two beautiful calendars, one for you and one for your mate. Schedule sex on your calendars.
2. Send your mate a small gift that relates to the evening you are planning.
3. Make the decision to do something spontaneous this week. Pay attention to your thoughts, and when you have a romantic thought, act on it *immediately*.
4. After you've read this chapter, you're sure to have some sexy thoughts this week. When it happens, be sure to call your mate and share it with him or her.
5. At least once this week, have a great time making love in a new place in your home.
6. Pick one of the adult encounters and try it out this week.

Six

DECORATING WITH
LOVE IN MIND

BUILD A LOVE NEST

Although you may be very adventurous and discover many other places in your house for making love, your bedroom is still the place you'll use the most. As your private domain and the place where you and your mate can be alone together to keep the fire lit, it is the most important room in your entire home. It's probably where your children were conceived, and it's a room that deserves your utmost attention. I used to ask the women in my class which room in their home had cost the most to decorate. Invariably, the answers would range from the living room to the dining room to the children's rooms, but never was it the master bedroom. Most people attach far more importance to the rooms where they entertain other people than to the room where they entertain themselves.

Since most children I know, including mine, spend very little time in their own room, forget the expense in making it a showplace. As far as the living room is concerned, your friends can sit on the floor with a few comfortable pillows around them. If money for decorating is limited, spend as much as you can afford on creating a private sanctuary for yourself and your mate where you can shut the door on the rest of the world, if only for a little while, and leave the rest of the decorating until finances permit.

FROM BEDROOM TO BOUDOIR

From now on, think of your bedroom as a boudoir—a room for romance—rather than just a place to sleep. If you have the budget to decorate with custom window and wall coverings, bedspreads, and such, hire a decorator. Usually, they don't charge for their time, because they make their money on your purchases, and together you can create a bedroom that reflects your taste but has the professional touch. Even if you can't afford expensive decorating, you can afford to do lots of things that will enhance your love nest.

LOCK IN YOUR PRIVACY

One of the most important and least expensive purchases you can make to guarantee your privacy is a lock for your bedroom door. Buy one that locks from the inside but has a key so that it can also be opened from the outside, in case the children should ever lock themselves in. The key can be hidden on the top of the doorjamb or somewhere where you, your mate, and other responsible adults know where to find it. Children can be taught at a very early age that when Mommy and Daddy's door is closed, it means they are having *private time*—a time when they want to be alone. Most of the time, you'll probably just be reading, watching TV, or talking. The important thing to get across to the children is that when that door is closed, you are not to be disturbed.

Don't worry if you feel guilty when you first start teaching your children to respect your privacy. I'd rather see you feel *guilty* about having your privacy than feel *resentment* for having no privacy. I'd rather see the children *resent* you in the beginning for shutting them out and feel *secure* later on because their parents love each other. I can't stress enough how important it is that, in the midst of this exhausting, hectic life, you and your mate can relax and enjoy yourselves in your bedroom sanctuary.

SOUNDS OF LOVE

Soundproofing your bedroom as much as possible is another important aspect of guaranteeing privacy. If you're worried about your children hearing the sounds of lovemaking that come from your bedroom, you'll never feel free to relax and enjoy yourselves. Most houses built in the last twenty years have acoustical ceilings that help deaden the sound. If you don't have an acoustical ceiling, invest in one. If you're building a new home, it's worth the extra cost to have bedroom walls fitted with double insulation. For maximum sound insulation, your bedroom must be carpeted. Even though hardwood floors are currently in style, your bedroom is *not* the place for them. Drapes are another soundproofing mechanism. Not only do they block out light, but they also absorb sound. If you have a headboard that bangs against the wall, consider attaching it to the wall permanently, or get a padded headboard that matches the decor of the room. And if your bed squeaks, get a new one.

YOUR BED

We spend about one third of our life in bed, sleeping. Add to that the countless hours we spend in bed relaxing, reading, napping, watching TV, talking on the telephone, communicating with our partners and, of course, making love, and you'll see that we spend more hours in bed than we do anywhere else. That's why it doesn't make sense to be stingy when it comes to buying your mattress. Mattresses are like carpets. You should always buy the very best that you can afford. Saving money by buying a cheap mattress isn't really very economical in the long run, when you consider the pain and expense of a bad back. Choosing the right mattress is very time-consuming, and what's exactly right for one person may be all wrong for another. When you go shopping for a mattress, don't be in a hurry. It may take you several shopping trips before you finally decide on the right one. Generally speaking, the firmer the mattress, the better it is for your back, but that's not always the case. There are lots of people who love waterbeds and who wouldn't buy anything else. If you have entertained the idea of a waterbed but aren't sure if you would like the effect, I suggest you go to a motel and try one out before making a commitment. If it feels good and you think it will have a positive effect on your lovemaking and your sleep, then by all means, indulge yourself.

SENSUAL SHEETS SPELL R-O-M-A-N-C-E

If you think the only reason to put sheets on the bed is to protect the mattress, think again. Your bed linens are as close to your skin as your lover's, and should be selected carefully to enhance your sensual experience. A moderate investment in the right kind of sheets can do more to create a feeling of luxury than just about anything else I can think of. And, like lovely lingerie, luxurious sheets can increase your feelings of romance and sexual excitement. Yes, fine sheets can be quite expensive, but they last a very long time. If you amortize the cost of the sheets over a period of, say, ten years, they end up costing very little per year. And the pleasure you'll get every time you slip between the sheets will be well worth the expense. The last thing you need or want is a rough, scratchy sheet, so be sure to consider color, texture, and pattern before buying. If you want the ultimate in sensuality, "go for the gold" and invest in satin sheets. Now that they've been perfected so that they can be laundered in your washer and dryer, you can be both practical and romantic. Other than satin sheets, the smoothest, softest sheets you can buy are 100 percent imported cotton, three-hundred-thread count. If these are still too expensive, two-hundred-thread count are also nice.

Just this year, my husband and I really splurged and bought all new bedding. We purchased a duvet, which is a goose-down comforter, along with a matching duvet cover and sheets of 100 percent imported cotton. Other than our spa, it was the best purchase we ever made. I can't believe we didn't do this years ago. Not a day goes by that I don't feel like a "princess" in my royal bed. Both my husband and I feel like we just melt into the covers. I, who used to love going to hotels, feel more comfortable and sexy in my own bed! Please don't make the mistake of waiting, as I did, before you treat yourself like royalty.

In the winter, cotton flannel sheets are soft and cozy, and they cost just a little more than the synthetics. Because they aren't slippery, they give good leverage, and as an added plus, they don't have to be ironed.

Canopy beds are a wonderful way to help you feel like royalty. They seem to create a "nest" where you can snuggle together and feel as though you are protected from the outside world. Draping the corners of the canopy bed with linens to match your sheets and pillowcases will give your room a "finished" look. If a canopy bed isn't feasible, but you like the idea of a nest, you can use drapery hardware and soft, billowing material to create a false canopy at the head of the bed.

DOUBLE YOUR PLEASURE WITH MIRRORS

Have you ever wondered why all the model homes you see have mirrored wardrobe doors, or whole walls of mirrors in the living room or dining room? It's because mirrors can make a room look much larger than it actually is. And a mirror has a way of expanding an experience as well as a room. Mirrors that reflect your sexual activity carry the psychological message that what goes on in the bedroom is worth looking at. As one of my students stated, "I'd rather look at my husband and me making love than

I would two strangers on a movie screen." If one of you is very conservative but the other is an exhibitionist at heart, the solution is simple. If you're conservative, don't look. If you're an exhibitionist, then by all means enjoy the view!

There are many ways to add mirrors to your private sanctuary without being as obvious as mounting them on the ceiling above your bed (although, if you aren't shy, you can certainly do so). Of course, mirrored wardrobe doors are a very acceptable part of bedroom decor, and if in the right place, can offer a very good view. Other solutions might be a mirrored headboard or light bridge, a triple mirror on the dresser opposite the bed, or a mirror mounted on the inside of the closet door that can be adjusted to reflect a most provocative image. There are even some bed frames that include a mirrored canopy over the bed! Any way you find to add mirrors to your lovemaking is fine, as long as it doubles your pleasure.

LIGHT UP YOUR LIFE

The proper lighting can do a great deal to enhance your appearance, as well as the appearance of your room. Even the most beautiful actress can look awful if the lighting isn't right, and the most ordinary person can look sensational with skillful lighting. That's why photographers, movie directors, and cinematographers will spend hours setting up the lighting for a scene or a photo shoot. Even a simple, inexpensive painting or poster has a dramatic effect given the proper lighting. To add drama to your bedroom, all you need are some spotlights strategically placed to highlight a portion of your room.

When you have more than reading on your mind, I recommend replacing your boring white light bulbs with *red* light bulbs. A red light can turn the most uninviting bedroom into a passionate hideaway, and it does wonders for your skin, giving you a more youthful appearance. For the ultimate in relaxation and romance, candlelight is a must. You can use anything from a single candle floating in a bowl of fresh gardenias to a lovely silver candelabra to cast your spell. Who knows, that mysteriously attractive stranger in your bed may turn out to be the very person you fell in love with before your children were even a gleam in your eye.

BREAKFAST IN BED

How you start the day can affect how your day goes, and even how it ends. Why hit the floor running when the alarm rings, if there's a way to linger in bed for a few minutes more as you prepare to meet the day? I think it's a lovely idea to have a bed tray in the bedroom, set with a pretty coffee or tea service, silver flatware, and linen napkins. A few cut flowers or a single fresh (or silk) rose will add the final touch. If you're a coffee drinker, there are small automatic coffeemakers with timers that you could place inconspicuously in your room. This way, you can have your coffee prepared and ready for you as you wake up in the morning. If you're a tea drinker, all you need is boiling water to brew you tea, an easy thing to accomplish with today's electric teakettles. No more dragging yourself to the kitchen and stumbling around with your eyes half-open, when your morning beverage is within arm's reach of your bed. You could even go a step further and leave muffins, tightly wrapped in plastic wrap or sealed in a plastic storage bag, on your bed tray. With a little planning, a small investment, and a few minutes' preparation before you retire for the evening, breakfast in bed can be an everyday luxury instead of an occasional treat, and the extra time you gain can be used to cuddle and chat.

A MINIBAR AT YOUR SERVICE

I believe that every love nest needs its own small refrigerator tucked away in the closet or an out-of-the-way corner of the bedroom. There's no reason to restrict your enjoyment of this extravagance to the times when you stay at a hotel. These refrigerators are available at most large discount outlets and are very affordable. With a refrigerator in the room, you can feel pampered anytime. Just think, you can keep it stocked with anything from sparkling cider to champagne; from simple snacks to special treats such as imported cheeses, smoked oysters, pâté de foie gras—even caviar. The finishing touch to your own private luxury suite is a silver tray attractively arranged with two crystal wineglasses, always ready to be used to toast your love.

MUSIC TO YOUR EARS

Music has been called the language of love. It has the power to evoke all kinds of feelings—from passion or romance to nostalgia or joy. A movie love scene devoid of music is unthinkable. Music sets the scene and creates the mood. Without music, everything would be flat and one-dimensional. For the ultimate experience, you and your mate need the right music for your own romantic rendezvous.

These days, many new homes come equipped with speakers in every room. But even if your home is older, you can still have great sound for a limited investment. One option is to have your house wired so that you can hook up an additional pair of speakers in your bedroom that will feed off of the amplifier in your living room or den. Another option is to get speakers that simply plug into your electrical outlet and work with an adapter from your main unit. Portable CD players, plugged into a portable stereo, can be hidden under the bed and will give excellent sound quality, or a portable cassette player can also be used.

The music you select is especially important. Music that is commonly referred to as "New Age" is especially soothing and relaxing, if that is what you like. If you feel more in the mood for something stimulating, a recording of Ravel's *Bolero* might be appropriate. Contemporary jazz offers some pleasant sounds, as do many of the classical selections. Some recording studios produce tapes, CD's, and records grouped together by category, such as "romantic music" or "music to make love by." What music you select is a personal choice. Discuss it with your mate and make a trip to a music store—another way to stimulate conversation and anticipation.

SCENT-SATIONAL BOUDOIRS

Our sense of smell is extremely powerful. Who hasn't had the experience of catching a whiff of freshly mown grass, night-blooming jasmine, or a sidewalk that has just been hosed down and been instantly and completely transported to another time and another place? So compelling is our sense of smell that it can trigger total recall of events that happened long, long ago.

The scent of fresh roses in your bedroom can signal that romance is in the air and put you in the mood for love instantly. If you can't afford a large bouquet, using one single flower in a bud vase can be just as effective. Floating a freshly picked gardenia in a clear glass bowl will fill the room with fragrance, or place a basket of oranges and lemons in a bowl on your night table for a refreshing scent. Scented candles, incense sticks, or a ring scented with oil are other ways to delight the sense of smell. Here's a clever tip: Fill the room with the scent of your favorite perfume by dabbing a small amount of the fragrance on an unlighted light bulb. When you turn on the light and the bulb heats up, it will diffuse the scent throughout the bedroom. You can also soak a cotton ball in perfume and tuck it into the corner of your drawer or the pillowcases on your bed. Scented drawer and shelf liners in various fragrances is also available, and looks as good as it smells. The idea is to leave behind the smells of detergents, cleaning agents, stale cooking odors, and tobacco smoke when you retreat to your private sanctuary.

While it won't replace your weekend getaway or your week's vacation without the children, a bedroom that has been transformed into a boudoir can offer you and your mate sanctuary every day from the trials and tribulations of parenting. Being good parents doesn't mean that you must always put *duty* before *pleasure*. In fact, the happier you are as a couple, the better you will be as parents. Your children can look after themselves while you take the time for sensual pleasure.

YOUR PRIVATE HEALTH SPA

There is another room in your home, besides your bedroom, where you should be able to enjoy privacy and a feeling of luxury, and that's the bathroom. In most homes, the bathroom is a constant source of irritation, rather than a pleasant place to retreat when the end of the day arrives and you want to unwind. For years I've had a chart in my classroom demonstrating how this tiny room is responsible for more arguments than any other room in the home. I'm sure that divorce on the grounds of "irreconcilable differences" really means that the couple couldn't agree on:

- Whether the toilet seat should be left up or down
- Where the toothpaste should be squeezed
- When to throw the toothpaste away
- Whether bath towels should be fresh every day or reused
- Whether the toilet paper should be rolled from the top or the bottom
- Which is better—showers or baths
- Whose job it is to squeegee the shower doors and wipe off the faucets

I'm sure you could add to the list, and even having "His" and "Hers" bathrooms wouldn't solve the problem, since you both occupy the same house and have opinions about what goes on there. But let's see how to turn this room of grievances into a room that provides relaxation, pleasure, and a feeling of luxury.

If your house has only one full bath, then it will have to serve double duty. In the early evening the bathroom can be a "family" room—a place where your children can have lots of fun and a special closeness with their parents. In the late evening, the "family" room can be transformed into a private spa—a place where you and your mate can have fun and a special closeness with each other.

To begin the transformation, put your bathroom lights on a dimmer switch. This way you can create a different atmosphere depending on the mood you're in. Or, for the ultimate mood setter, forget the lights completely and use candles instead. There is no way to describe how sensual and peaceful the flickering of candlelight can be as you soak in a tub of warm water laced with your favorite bath salts.

Next, consider spending a little more money for your towels. Inexpensive towels are often rough to the touch and are too small to be efficient. On the other hand, a more expensive towel has a deep pile that's soft to the touch and is large enough to wrap you in a cocoon of luxury.

If your bathroom is very small, consider covering one or two walls with mirrors to make it appear larger. Another nice touch is to replace the cheap chrome fixtures with custom fixtures that complement your decor. If your home has a country theme, use brass and wood, or brass and porcelain, fixtures. If you have a more modern decor, go for the sleek Eurostyle look. New fixtures will give your home the look of a custom home and create an illusion of wealth for a fairly small expenditure.

Use plants to dress up your bathroom inexpensively. They thrive in the moist atmosphere and can turn any bathroom into a garden of beauty.

Buy attractive "His" and "Hers" spa robes. These thick terry-cloth robes will give you both years of pleasure and can be hung in plain sight on oversized decorative hooks as a daily reminder that when the children are out of the way, the adults can play!

A shower radio is a nice addition to your private spa. As the playwright Congreve said, "Music hath charms to soothe the savage breast." It is also a wonderful way to soothe the soul of the average harassed parent.

Take some time to investigate a bath shop or a shop that specializes in lotions, potions, and sweet-smelling things. If you buy a little each time, before you know it, you'll have a collection of powders, creams, lotions, soaps, bubble bath, and oils. Keep all of your personal items in a pretty basket or a special box, or cover a hatbox with fabric to match your bathroom decor and use it to store them.

If you have a large master bathroom separate from the children's bath, a nice addition is an oversized round ottoman upholstered to match your decor. Besides being a convenient place to paint your toenails or put on your stockings, this portable piece of furniture can be an exciting springboard to experimentation. Just let your imagination be your guide.

TURN ON THE WATER AND TURN ON

Although it's never been the subject of serious study, I'm convinced that people have more flashes of insight and creativity while shaving, showering, or soaking in the tub than anyplace else. There have been many times when the bathroom has been my "think tank." Maybe the running water acts as a form of hypnosis, relaxing us enough that our minds are free to go to a higher consciousness.

Besides quieting our minds, water relaxes our bodies, making it a very effective aphrodisiac. For most of us, the easiest way to enjoy the benefits of water is in our own shower or bathtub. But if you haven't discovered the pleasure of swimming in the nude with your mate, you've missed out on a very sensual experience. Embracing takes on a whole new dimension when your nude bodies are immersed in water. Your hands glide over each other's skin, which feels like velvet. Not only that, but in water, we lose 90 percent of our body weight. So, for those of us who are self-conscious about our weight, here is the perfect way to feel light as a feather. In water, any man can feel strong and masculine as he carries his mate with the support of the water. You just might feel dainty and light for the first time in your life as you lock your arms around his neck and your legs around his waist. Skinny-dipping in a swimming pool, ocean, hot tub, Jacuzzi, lake, or river with only the moonlight illuminating your bodies is an exquisite experience that cannot be equaled.

ASSIGNMENT #6

Becoming a Better Parent

1. Have your children make a Do Not Disturb sign to hang on your bedroom door and let them make one for their room, too. Respect their privacy by giving them an opportunity to have alone time in their own room once in a while.

2. Sit down with your children and plan some activities that they can do quietly alone, while you enjoy yourselves behind closed doors. You may want to purchase some special games and activity books (stickers, paint-by-numbers) that they can play with unsupervised and save these for your "private times."

3. Children should read more. If your children are old enough to read, take them to the library every week and stock up on books. Then, instead of watching TV, they can read their books, while you are in your own "reading room."

Becoming a Better Partner

1. Start a file folder dedicated to your boudoir. Collect pictures and ideas from magazines that are representative of the setting you want to create. A magazine called *Victoria* is an excellent source of romantic settings.

2. If you don't have a lock on your bedroom door, get one installed this week.

3. Go to a bath shop this week and buy one or two items for your personal collection of bath accessories.

4. Try one of the decorating tips for your bedroom or bathroom to make it more private and romantic.

Seven

NOT TONIGHT, DEAR, THERE'S A CHILD IN OUR BED!

TO SHARE OR NOT TO SHARE (YOUR BED)

There are at least two separate and distinct schools of thought as to whether a child should be allowed to share his parents' bed. While both schools of thought are concerned with what's best for the child, experts on one side say that a child should never, under any circumstances, be allowed to sleep with his parents, and experts on the other side say that it is perfectly all right for a child to share his parent's bed for as long as necessary. Once again, I believe that what's best for the child is to have parents who love each other, so my answer to the dilemma rests with what is best for the parents.

Anyone who has raised a child knows it's difficult, if not impossible, to deal with absolutes. While it's important to have rules and set standards for behavior, when it comes to raising children, it's even more important to be flexible. Parents who are so rigid that they can never bend a rule are bound to drive themselves crazy. *Always* and *never* are terms that can get you in a lot of trouble when it comes to parenting. Personally, I feel that there is nothing wrong with having your child sleep in your bed from time to time. Sometimes it's the *only* way you can get any sleep at all. There were many nights when I decided that crowding into one bed was easier to take than constantly getting up to deal with a fearful or ill child. Most parents who have raised healthy, happy kids will admit that there was a time when each of their children had a need to climb into their bed.

It is not wrong to let a child come into your bed and to hold him tightly or stroke him and let him feel comforted by your body next to his. The desire to comfort and nurture our children is quite powerful, and it's all right to follow our instinct to hold and comfort our child when we feel the need to do so. But there's a big difference between sharing your bed *sometimes* and sharing your bed *all the time*. I never thought twice about taking our children into bed with us when they were scared or sick. In a few days, however, the cold cleared up, the diaper rash disappeared, the tooth finally cut through the gums, the fever was gone, the nightmare was forgotten, the monsters went away, and it was time for the child to return to his own bed. My husband always understood that the child in our bed was there temporarily, and he never resented postponing our intimate time together for the sake of our children. He knew that when the child returned to his own room, we could focus on each other again.

Parents who tend to think in terms of black and white, always and never, or right and wrong, may worry that if they allow their child into their bed sometimes, the child will expect to be held, cuddled, and allowed to sleep in their bed all of the time. I don't think this needs to be the case. Letting the children sleep with us occasionally wasn't a problem for us, and it wasn't a problem for hundreds of other parents I've spoken with. Setting limits and being clear, in our own minds, about our feelings sets the tone for our children. We are the ones in charge, not our children. While our children may have been welcome in our bed when they were needy, my husband and I made it clear that this was not going to be an everyday occurrence. We had our bed, and they had theirs.

THREE'S A CROWD

For years I've heard the complaint, mostly from men, that once their child started sharing their bed, their sex life became nonexistent. These men felt robbed of the tender, loving moments that they used to enjoy with their mates before the child came into their bed.

One night in class a student named Eric volunteered that he resented the fact that his son was coming into bed with him and his wife every night. "Don't get me wrong," Eric said. "I love my son, but enough is enough. I thought it was cute in the beginning, but I feel so distant from my wife lately. Before Jamie was born, we used to cuddle every night. Now the only one getting cuddled is Jamie."

Curt confided that his daughter has been sleeping with him and his wife for the last two years. "She started coming into our room when she was three," he said. "My wife insisted that she was frightened and needed to be with us, and I went along with her, thinking it would just be for a short time. I had no idea that we'd be a threesome every single night. I really can't stand it anymore. I can't remember the last time I saw my wife in a negligee."

Another student said his five-year-old son had been in their bed since birth. "I can't take it anymore," he said in total frustration. "We never make love anymore. The only thing we use our bed for is sleep."

Fortunately, the wives of these three men took my class after their husbands completed theirs. They came to realize that while they were catering to their children's needs, they had forgotten about their husband's needs. They felt, as so many women do, that their husband's needs could wait but their children's couldn't. It's so easy for a woman to become so involved in nurturing her children while ignoring her mate that, before she knows it, her relationship with her partner is destroyed.

Women are not the only ones who are guilty of putting more emphasis on the children than on the relationship. Some men have a sense that now that their mates are mothers, it's not okay to think of them sexually. Others fall into the same patterns that their wives do, and put all of their time and energy into parenting. It's not uncommon for men (and women, too) to want to be better parents than their own were, and this is great. But all too often, in an attempt to become "Superdad" or "Supermom," these parents lose sight of their relationship with each other. In both my men's and women's courses, I have always emphasized that *the relationship between a man and a woman must be stronger and of a higher priority than the relationship between parent and child.*

When the child is the center of attention, everyone,

including the child, suffers. Without realizing it—little by little, day by day—the mother loses her identity as a woman, wife, and lover. Consequently, her husband becomes resentful toward her and the child. He then becomes distant, uncooperative, and angry. Eventually, the family unit breaks down, and the possibility of divorce becomes a reality. Unless guarded against, the birth of a baby often destroys the intimacy in a relationship and may lead to a husband's first episode of infidelity.

I promise every young parent reading this book that your baby will eventually sleep through the night and his or her schedule will become less demanding. Soon your child will learn how to dress himself, feed himself, and go off to school by himself. Eventually, there will come a day when he will leave home to begin life on his own. No matter how wonderful your relationship with your child is, remind yourself that he will leave you. I know that a baby can satisfy your physical need to touch as you bathe, powder, dress, carry, kiss, and hold her. I am aware that more and more men are beginning to share these tasks and that sometimes their sexual desire is turned off as they get into the role of "Daddy." Please look at the partner by your side, who really wants to stay with you forever. Reach out for your mate's physical closeness and don't rely so heavily on your child. Although the sheer physical pleasure of snuggling, caressing, rubbing, tickling, nibbling, and holding that was once reserved for just the two of you is now shared with a child, you must make an effort to recapture or retain that intimacy with each other. You must:

- Cuddle with each other—not just the child
- Stroke each other—not just the child

- Kiss each other—not just the child
- Sleep with each other—not just the child

For many people, making the transition from being totally involved with your child to feeling sexy once again is very difficult. Fear of another pregnancy, fear of painful intercourse, a deep sense of fulfillment in your role as mother or father, can make it easy to use the child as an excuse to avoid sex, but it cannot be put on hold forever. You must stay romantically connected to your mate if you wish to preserve your relationship.

WE CAN DO *WHAT*?

"Well, what did the doctor say?" my husband asked eagerly after my six-week postnatal checkup. I think it's the only time in the history of our marriage that I wanted to lie. My first inclination was to say, "The doctor said it would be a good year or two before we could make love again." Instead, I heard myself telling my husband the truth. "He said everything looked great, and we could have sex any time we wanted to," I reluctantly admitted.

Is there a woman anywhere who doesn't remember how she felt when she heard those comforting words from her physician, "You can resume sex in six weeks"? The women in my class and I have shared many a laugh as we discovered our similar reactions. Here are just a few examples of a typical response (whether verbalized or not) when a woman hears those words:

"You've got to be kidding."
"You're joking, right?"

"How much did my husband pay you to say that?"

"Your wife may be Superwoman, but I'm not."

"Sex. What's that?"

"Please don't repeat that to my husband."

"I don't have the strength to do more than collapse from exhaustion."

There are many reasons why sex is usually the furthest thing from a woman's mind after giving birth.

- Her hormones can change, causing a diminished sex drive.
- She had a difficult labor or a painful episiotomy. After childbirth, it's hard to believe anything to do with your genitals could feel good.
- She's physically exhausted from lack of sleep. Nursing mothers are especially tired, since they can't share the responsibility of nighttime feedings with anyone.
- She may suffer from postpartum depression.

All of these conditions are temporary, and each woman will have her own timetable for recovery. While she's experiencing them, a woman may, at an unconscious level, use the child as an excuse to avoid sex. Although she may genuinely believe that letting the child share their bed is in the child's best interest, subconsciously she may want to discourage any sexual advances from her husband. Time alone and physical contact with each other are important at every stage of your life together. In time your desire for sex will return, but in the meantime, don't rob yourself and your mate of the intimacy that is so vital to your relationship.

Women: Allow your mate the pleasure of holding,

cuddling, and stroking you even if you're not ready for sex.

Men: Give your mate the pleasure of being held, cuddled, and stroked without pressuring her for sex.

Not only will having a child in your bed prevent you from making love, it will also prevent you from even beginning the transition from being parents to being lovers again. After all, there are some things you just won't do if a child is present.

FIFTEEN THINGS YOU WON'T DO IF THERE IS A CHILD IN YOUR BED

1. Watch an adult movie.
2. Give each other a massage.
3. Kiss passionately.
4. Make love.
5. Sleep in each other's arms.
6. Sleep in the nude.
7. Play an erotic game.
8. Sleep on satin sheets.
9. Have a pillow fight.
10. Tickle each other.
11. Wear a sexy negligee.
12. Stroke each other as you plan and dream about the future.
13. Eat munchies while watching TV.
14. Slow-dance to romantic music.
15. Talk "dirty" to each other.

YOU AND YOU ALONE

One of the greatest pleasures we have as parents is the sense of awe and fulfillment we feel as we hold our baby and rock it to sleep. If you fall into the trap of always holding your child until he is asleep and then putting him down, you're training your child to rely on you to *put* him to sleep, instead of training him to fall asleep on his own. Before you establish a habit of *putting* your child to sleep, consider the consequences of training your child to *need* your physical presence in order to fall asleep.

Art and Toby's daughter Suzie had slept with them since birth. One night, when Suzie was eighteen months old, Art had to be rushed to the hospital with an attack of appendicitis. In a panic, Toby called a neighbor to come over to watch Suzie while she took her husband to the hospital. "His appendix had ruptured, and he had to have an emergency appendectomy," Toby recalls. "I stayed the whole night waiting for the results of the surgery," she said. "Finally, when I knew he was resting comfortably, I went home. When I arrived, I was shocked to find Suzie crying hysterically and my neighbor blurry-eyed and apologetic. Suzie had awakened in the middle of the night, and without us beside her she couldn't go back to sleep. Nothing my neighbor did could calm Suzie down. It was then that I realized that my daughter had to learn to sleep by herself or we'd never be able to leave her."

Marie was another woman who knew that she needed to retrain her nine-month-old son. "I'm afraid I've robbed myself of the possibility of having any social life ever again," she complained to the class. "I didn't mind giving up our nightlife for the sake of our son at first. He was such a demanding child from the very beginning that it seemed like putting him in bed with us was the right thing to do. Now I realize what a mistake that was. Last month I felt I just had to get out. We hadn't been out to a movie, a restaurant, or even a friend's house in the eight months since Eric's birth. We hired a baby-sitter and planned to go to dinner and a movie. I called home after dinner to see how things were going and found out that the situation at home was a total disaster. No matter what the sitter did—and believe me, she tried everything—Eric wouldn't stop crying. We had to skip the movie and go straight home," Marie said.

Most new parents don't mind sacrificing evenings out, believing, like Marie, that it's strictly a temporary state of affairs. However, for many parents the days turn into weeks, the weeks turn into months, the months turn into years, and these unfortunate parents are trapped in an arrangement they don't know how to change.

Most parents who bring their child into bed with them do so in a misguided attempt to get the child to sleep through the night. However, most children do wake up at least once or twice during the night. Rather than worry about whether he'll wake up or not, your goal should be to have your child become independent enough that he doesn't need your help to go back to sleep when he does awaken. Only by recognizing that it is your child's responsibility to fall asleep and get back to sleep on his own can you reclaim your social life, your sex life, and your own restful sleep.

If you've already established a pattern of *putting* your child to sleep, you must break the pattern. Children learn quickly, and if you're motivated enough to hang in there even though it's agonizing, earsplitting, or aggravating, you'll be surprised at how fast you can turn the situation around. I've talked to many, many parents to learn what techniques they've used to help their children sleep on their own. Most of their suggestions were based on the same techniques that have been used for years, the simple ways parents have always had of comforting a child and making him feel secure. Now you can learn from the experts—parents who have successfully weaned their children from dependence to self-reliance.

TEDDY BEARS AND BLANKETS

Providing a child with a stuffed animal or security blanket was by far the most common way parents suggested to comfort children and get them to sleep on their own. Rather than comforting your child with your presence, comfort your child with a special blanket or a teddy bear. Vicky said, "I always tuck Tina, my three-year-old, and her teddy bear into bed together. This way, when Tina wakes up during the night, *Teddy* will help comfort her back to sleep. With Teddy on duty, my husband and I are comfortable leaving Tina with a baby-sitter, because Teddy is all Tina needs to fall back asleep."

An enlightened father, Howie says, "Growing up isn't easy. If a security blanket or teddy bear can make life easier for my son, then why not? I guess some men are afraid of having their son look like a sissy, but I'm convinced that my son feels more secure having his special blanket. I figure when he's old enough, he'll let go of the blanket on his own. In the meantime, he gets a good night's sleep, and so do his mother and I."

To comfort a newborn, you must reassure him in some way that his mother is nearby. Familiar smells and familiar sounds are often reassuring. Diapers that have become burp rags often become the treasured bit of cloth that spells comfort to the baby and R-E-L-I-E-F to the frazzled dad, grandparent, or baby-sitter. Familiar soft noises are another way to reassure an infant. I remember the time, when I was a child, that we got a very young puppy. We had a marvelous time fixing a nice warm bed out of a cardboard box and some old blankets. We loved holding this soft, silky little darling and watching her clumsy antics as she tried to crawl in and out of her box. But that night, all the fun of the afternoon was replaced by a desperate need to find a way to stop the puppy's constant, unrelenting whining. That's when my mother remembered a trick she had learned when she had gotten her first puppy as a child. Mom found an old alarm clock, wound it up tight, and placed it in a corner of the box under a blanket.

"The puppy hears the clock ticking and thinks it's her mother's heartbeat," my mom explained. Sure enough, the puppy put her little head down and slept quietly the rest of the night.

Now, decades later, this old concept has been incorporated into a new product for newborns. Called "Rock-A-Bye Bunny" or "Rock-A-Bye Bear," it duplicates the sounds heard by the infant in the womb, including the sound of a heartbeat, as well as a swishing sound. Another new product is "Snuggle Heads," an arc stuffed with poly-cotton that fits snugly around the infant's head, creating the same sense of security he experienced in the mother's womb.

BE A BORE

One woman I interviewed said that she had never had a problem with her two-year-old son until he learned how to climb out of his crib. "Tommy was coming into our room at least four or five times a night," she revealed. "I was so worn out from lack of sleep that I was a zombie at work. Every time I had to get up and put Tommy back to bed, it took me at least twenty minutes to get back to sleep. So usually, after four or five attempts at getting him to stay in his crib, Tommy would wind up in our bed. Finally, I made up my mind that this just had to end. I decided to devote an entire week to solving the problem. *Every* time Tommy came into our room, I simply returned him to his crib without reacting to him. He got no more smiles, no more sympathy, and no more hugs in the middle of the night. It was tough, but it was worth it," Heidi said. "By the end of the week Tommy stayed in his crib all night and didn't get up at all. I was able to be effective at work again, and I was a better mom, too, because I was getting some much-needed sleep. Our sex life improved, too, once we knew Tommy wasn't going to keep popping into our room."

The following list of "Don'ts" was compiled after interviewing many moms and dads who were successful at having a child sleep in his own bed. Keep in mind that you can do all of these things at other times, but once your child has been put to bed for the night, the fun is over. Allow at least half an hour for a bedtime ritual, kiss your child good-night, and then:

• Don't give hugs and kisses.
• Don't read him another story.
• Don't sing him another song.
• Don't rock him again.
• Don't give him another glass of water.
• Don't give him sympathy.

- Don't give him your attention.
- Don't apologize.
- Don't argue.
- Don't give an explanation.
- Don't beg.

Don't make it rewarding for your child to get out of his bed and come into yours. Don't entertain him, and don't socialize with him in the middle of the night. In other words, be a complete bore.

REWARD GOOD BEHAVIOR

Rewarding good behavior is a proven method for ensuring that it will be repeated. There are many types of rewards, from an appreciative comment to a hug and kiss to a much-wanted toy. Cari recommended her reward system to the class. "I used a star chart to help my children stay in their beds," she said. "Every night that they stayed in bed, they got a gold star. When they were able to stay three nights in a row, I took them to the store where they were allowed to pick out a small toy. If they got a gold star every day for a week, they could pick out something larger. If they got gold stars for a whole month, then they could select a bigger toy. At that point, the behavior was usually permanent. It was a little expensive, but it was worth it to me. I used this method happily and successfully with all four of my kids, even though one of my friends accused me of bribing my children and thought it was wrong. It was a great system. The children felt good about themselves because they were able to sleep by themselves, I felt good because I was rested, and my husband and I had the opportunity to maintain a great sex life."

TO NAP OR NOT TO NAP?

Sometimes the solution to getting a child to sleep through the night in his own bed is as simple as eliminating or limiting a nap. Carlotta, an elementary school teacher, was a little embarrassed when she told the class her baby-sitter had pointed out the solution to her daughter's sleep problem. "I'm still learning that each of my children has different needs," said Carlotta. "I never had a problem with Matthew, my five-year-old, going to sleep and staying asleep. But my two-year-old daughter, Lisa, was a different story. While my husband and I were ready to collapse by ten in the evening, Lisa was still wide awake. When she finally did go to sleep, she'd be up at least three or four times during the night and always wanted to sleep in our bed. When I told my sitter the problem, she suggested that maybe Lisa could take one nap at midday, instead of taking a morning and afternoon nap, as she had been doing. I know this sounds simple, but it solved our problem. Lisa can hardly keep her eyes open after seven o'clock now. She's in bed by eight, and my husband and I are rediscovering each other. What a pleasure it is to have uninterrupted adult conversation and privacy once again," Carlotta concluded.

TRY THE RATIONAL APPROACH

A student named Don used a method that I thought was brilliant. He shared his solution one night in class. "We never had a problem with Danny's sleeping habits until he was about five years old. Then, all of a sudden, he started coming up with every excuse in the book as to why he wasn't sleepy. Even after we'd finally get him to sleep, he'd get up two or three times a night wanting to come into our bed. For about six months, Danny was definitely in charge and controlling us. When I just couldn't stand it anymore, I sat down with Danny one night and told him we had a new rule. I explained to him how it was important for him to get a least eleven hours of sleep every night, and that I was very concerned that he was not getting enough rest. I told him that until he could get to sleep faster and stay in bed all night, he had to go to bed at seven o'clock to make up for the sleep he was losing every night. It only took a week for Danny to stay in his bed when we put him to bed at seven and not come into our bed at all. As soon as he was able to stay in his bed, he got his eight o'clock bedtime back, and my wife and I had our time to be alone back."

BE IMAGINATIVE

When I put my children to bed at night, I used to tell them to close their eyes because the sandman was coming to put them to sleep. "You can't see him because he's invisible," I told them, "but he sprinkles your eyes with magical stardust to make them sleepy." Then I'd sing a song to them about the sandman.

Ben, a student in one of my classes, said that when he tucked his daughter in at night, he'd go through an enormous list of who else was going to sleep now, along with his daughter. The list included Cinderella, Snow White, and Bambi, to name just a few. Then Ben added uncles, aunts, cousins, friends, teachers, and neighbors. Obviously, this nightly ritual meant a great deal to his daughter, because now that she has a child of her own, she does the same thing. "It was such a peaceful, private time we shared," Ben said. "Bedtime was always a very happy, imaginative time," he said, "a time when everyone everywhere looked forward to going to sleep."

As a rule, children love rituals and are comforted by having a set routine around bedtime. Bedtime stories, lullabies, prayers, and familiar sayings like "Sleep tight. Don't let the bedbugs bite" all serve as ways to calm your child and get him ready for sleep.

SET LIMITS NOW FOR SECURITY LATER

Remember, there's nothing intrinsically wrong with your child's sleeping in your bed from time to time. Having your child in bed with you can be a warm and wonderful experience. It's when the practice disrupts your sleep and your intimacy with your mate that it becomes a problem. My husband and I still cherish the times when our children shared our bed. In recent years, one of the highlights of the summer has been when our daughter crawls into our bed the morning before she returns to college and gives us a big hug.

It's normal for infants to awaken frequently for nighttime feeding, but most of them sleep through the night by six months of age. If your child is older than six months and is still keeping you up at night, or if your child sleeps in your bed most of the time, you and the child have a problem. In this chapter, we have talked about a few of the ways you might use to return your child to his bed, where he belongs, and reclaim your bed for your and your mate's exclusive pleasure and rest.

ASSIGNMENT #7

Becoming a Better Parent

1. Set a new bedtime routine that starts at least a half hour before you turn off the lights.
2. Enlist your child's help. Ask her what could be done so that she doesn't come into your bed anymore. You may be surprised at the solutions offered. One child said he wanted to sleep in the same room as his older sister. The parents took his suggestion and moved his bed into his sister's room. Now everyone is sleeping peacefully.
3. Give your child a security blanket, stuffed animal, flashlight, or night-light to help him feel more secure.
4. Build positive feelings about your child's bed and bedroom. Ask him what you could do to make his room a happier, more comfortable place to sleep. One child said that as long as the door stayed open and a light was on in the hallway, he'd feel safe.
5. Sometimes a child's sleep problems are more difficult to handle and cannot be corrected without the help of a qualified expert. If you've tried everything and the problem persists, consult your pediatrician.

Becoming a Better Partner

1. Pick a time when you and your mate can talk about the problem of the child in your bed in a focused way. Explain how important it is to you to have uninterrupted sleep and a place where you can have a sense of privacy. Decide on a plan of action that you can both support and implement.

2. Set a deadline for reclaiming your bed for cuddling, holding, stroking, and relaxing, based on your action plan.

3. Using a "Fireworks" sticker, schedule a date on your calendar for you and your mate to have a slumber party for two. Plan to enjoy yourselves in your private sanctuary with no interruptions from your children.

4. Review "Fifteen Things You Won't Do If There Is a Child in Your Bed," and enjoy at least two of the activities listed there.

Eight

HOUSEWORK IS
A TEAM EFFORT

WHO DOES WHAT?

For some couples, deciding who does what in the home can be a big problem. They argue over who's going to clean, cook, take the car in for repairs, take the kids to day care, and on and on. In our family, there's never been a problem with regard to housework, for three important reasons. First, my husband and I have always been committed to doing whatever is necessary to make the other's life easier. Second, each of us really appreciates what the other does, and we never take each other for granted. And last but not least, we constantly verbalize our appreciation and tell each other what a great job we're doing.

In addition, gender has never been a factor in who does a particular job in our house. If my husband is away on a business trip, I take over all the chores and errands. If I'm away, my husband takes over. Since I was busy in the evenings teaching my classes for more than ten years, my husband was the one who helped the children with their homework, served them the dinner that I had prepared, cleaned up the kitchen, and put the children to bed. Since I was home during the day, I'm the one who went shopping for groceries, did all the necessary errands, and saw to it that the children went off to school on time.

We looked at housework as something that simply needed to be done, and we divided it up. When the children were old enough, they began to help and do their part. As they grew, their responsibilities increased. They were raised with the understanding that as family members they had to do their fair share. They understood that nobody got a "free ride." As a result, my nineteen-year-old son can cook, clean, and do laundry just as well as his two sisters. Going off to college and being on their own was not difficult for any of my children because they had pulled their own weight and learned independence at home. Now that all of our children are out of the house, my husband and I are back to sharing the work load between the two of us. More often than not, we go to the supermarket together, straighten up the house together, make the bed together, and even cook together.

Does having a husband and children who routinely do their share of the housework sound too good to be true? Well, believe it or not, it is possible to have a balanced division of labor in the home, and I'm going to teach you how to achieve it. In this chapter, you will learn how to run your home so that it's better organized, more efficient, and most important of all, a happier place to live.

SO MUCH WORK, SO LITTLE TIME

Housework is a never-ending necessity. No matter how hard you work, you'll always be behind. As the comedian Phyllis Diller once said, "I'm eighteen years behind in my ironing. There's no use doing it now. It doesn't fit anybody I know!" And, with more than 50 percent of women now working outside the home, the old adage "Man may work from sun to sun, but a woman's work is never done" is truer than ever. While we are on the subject of work, let's get something straight. Every wife and mother works, whether she is employed outside the home or not. A full-time homemaker and a woman who is employed outside the home are both just as exhausted at the end of a day, and both deserve to relax and have some time to themselves. When Irwin, an executive with a large computer firm, complained about his wife one night in class, it was clear that he didn't understand this.

"I've had it," Irwin said. "I work hard all day and expect to be able to come home and relax. But my wife is too busy to relax with me. She doesn't get the kids to bed until ten o'clock at night, and then she spends another hour cleaning the kitchen and straightening up the house. All I want is to watch some TV in peace and quiet, have a conversation with my wife, and read the newspaper."

When I suggested that his wife needed his help, he looked puzzled. "Why should I have to help?" he asked. "I work ten hours a day every day of the week, and she's home all day doing nothing." I assured him that with four children under the age of nine, his wife was not doing nothing. In fact, his wife had just finished taking the women's class, so I knew her day began at six in the morning and didn't end until 11:00 P.M. In reality, she was working seventeen hours a day. Like so many women in my classes, Greta was afraid to confront Irwin about the help she needed from him for fear of driving him away. What she didn't realize was that her lack of sexual desire and her constant exhaustion were what was driving a wedge between them, not the fact that she needed his help. After discussing the situation with him, I gave Irwin two choices if he wanted to save his marriage. He could either hire outside help, or he could help his wife with the work on a daily basis. Feeling that outside help was beyond their budget, Irwin chose the latter. By helping Greta with the evening chores and getting the kids off to bed, Irwin cut her evening work load in half. Now everything is done by nine o'clock, and after two weeks of the new routine, Greta called to thank me for giving her fourteen extra hours a week. By the end of the men's class, Irwin admitted that he was thrilled to have a wife he could talk to, relax with, and make love to once again.

I NEED HELP

It's surprising how many women are reluctant to ask for their mate's help with the housework. They still believe—consciously or unconsciously—that housework is a woman's job and that somehow it's unfair to expect their husband or mate to share the responsibility. Whenever we talk about housework in my women's class, I know what to expect. I've heard every excuse in the book from women who have told me why they can't ask their mates for help. The main reasons women don't ask for help are:

- They feel guilty asking.
- They believe doing housework is their job.
- They don't want to make their husband angry.
- It's too much trouble to ask.
- No one will clean like they clean.

For example, Charlene said she feels guilty. "I saw my mom do everything in my family when I was growing up. Our house was always spotless. Mom used to brag that people could eat off the floors. Well, you can eat off my floors, too. You can eat spaghetti in one corner and hamburger in the other. Even though I only work part time and am home every day by two o'clock, I can't seem to get it together. I know I should be able to manage my part-time job and my home, but I find having a two-year-old is overwhelming. But I just can't ask my husband for help. He puts in long hours at work trying to get ahead financially, and I feel too guilty asking for his help."

"It's my job," a woman named Meg asserted one night. "My husband takes out the garbage, mows the lawn, pays the bills, and takes care of the car. It's my job to cook, clean, do the shopping, and take care of the kids. It's true, I don't have a moment to myself, but that's what happens when you have a family. I'm certainly not going to ask him to do my job."

"My mate will get annoyed," said Anita. "If I ask him to do more around the house, he'll get mad and tell me that he's already doing his share by working eight hours a day to support us. I'd rather have peace and quiet and try to run the home myself than to have him get mad at me," she confided. "I don't like his disapproval."

"It's such a hassle to ask for help," Pat confessed. "I used to have my husband help, but I'd have to remind him over and over before he'd finally get around to doing what he agreed to do. It got to be such a hassle that it just seemed easier to do it myself."

Sybil worried that no one would clean as well as she does. "You don't know my husband," she volunteered. "If I ask him to vacuum, for example, he skips an entire area. His idea of cleaning the kitchen is to stack the dirty dishes in the sink. Wiping the countertops or sweeping the floor never even occurs to him."

All of these women thought they had valid reasons for not asking for help. But, interestingly enough, they all admitted that they felt resentful, angry, exhausted, and sexually unresponsive. In reality, they were damaging their relationships far more by being martyrs than they would be by asking for help. As a result of the class, these women, and others like them, were able to come to the realization that asking for help around the house was in *everyone's* best interests. They also learned skills that increased their chances of getting the help they needed.

Charlene learned to ask for help, despite her feelings of guilt. As she began to expect less from herself and ask more from her husband, they both experienced the intimacy that comes from truly sharing in a relationship. Meg learned that gender did not have to define a particular chore. Her husband actually loved to cook, but never had the opportunity because Meg had defined it as a "woman's job." In turn, Meg found she enjoyed washing the car, which she had avoided in the past because she considered it a "man's job." Meg and her husband discovered that they actually enjoyed taking over each other's jobs. These days, you'll find Meg's husband shopping for groceries and Meg mowing the lawn. Sharing in all the responsibilities has given them a new closeness.

When Anita became aware that her disinterest in sex was a direct result of her resentment toward her husband for his lack of support, she took the chance and asked for help despite her fear of rocking the boat. When she explained to her husband that one of the reasons she was uninterested in making love was because she was always tired, he began to take on more responsibility.

When Sybil learned that her husband had stopped helping around the house because all he received for his efforts was ridicule and criticism, she took a good look at her need to control and began to relax her standards a little. With some encouragement and praise, Sybil's husband began to take on more responsibility, and Sybil's load lifted.

Pat learned that if she let her husband choose which chores he wanted to do from a list of those that needed to be done, he was much more willing and responsible.

TEAMWORK

Any basketball player can tell you that you can win more games by passing the ball than by trying to score all the points yourself. Well, a family is a team, too. To manage the household more easily, each family member should be recognized as an important team member. Just like in any team sport, each player has a job to do. If one member drops the ball, it hurts the whole team. On the other hand, when everybody does his job, everybody wins!

"Many hands make light work," and dividing the chores among all family members benefits everyone by giving them more leisure time to enjoy family. To get everyone to pitch in and work as a team may take some effort and creativity, but it's worth it.

The first step in rallying your team behind you is to make a list of all the chores involved in running a household. Begin with broad categories, and then under each category list each individual job. Next to each job note the amount of time each member of the family contributes to that job. Having everything down in black and white will make it very clear to everyone exactly what it takes to run the house and the current division of labor.

Use the following charts as examples, filling in the time spent according to your own situation. These charts should be customized to fit your particular needs. Don't forget how many hours you spend working outside the home. If you have the added responsibility of caring for elderly parents, add that to your list. Remember, the more complete and detailed your list is, the easier it is to see if everyone is pulling his weight, and it will be clear who needs to do more.

YOUR MAN'S SUPPORT

The next step in implementing a team approach to running the house is to arrange for a discussion with your mate. Believe it or not, most men can be convinced to do their fair share in running a household if—and it's a big if—they are approached in a loving,

Is There Sex After Kids? 191

calm, rational way. Screaming, "What do I have to do to get help around here?" or "Am I the only one living in this house?" will not elicit cooperation. Presenting your plan when one or the other of you is in a rush or likely to be distracted is not very effective, either. Plan to set aside an evening or a time on the weekend when you can talk uninterrupted and without feeling pressured. Maybe you could talk over a cup of coffee on the patio, or go out for a drive together. Marla, one of my students, was very surprised to see how such a simple technique could work so well. She told me that she and her husband made a date to go to a neighborhood restaurant where they would have privacy and the necessary time to talk. "Instead of my usual screaming and carrying on, I calmly explained to him that I didn't want to be the one exclusively in charge of chores. I had taken your advice and listed all of the chores on a chart. I asked my husband to read it, and when he was done, I looked at him lovingly and said, "I really want to spend less time on chores, so that I can pay more attention to you." His immediate response was "How can I help?"

Preparing Meals	Self	Mate	Child 1	Child 2
Planning				
Shopping				
Cooking				
Setting the table				
Serving				
Clearing the table				
Washing the dishes				
Putting away the dishes				

Packing lunches _____

Cleaning House—This one can be broken down into individual rooms, i.e., living room, dining room, master bedroom, second bedroom, third bedroom, bathroom, and kitchen. Then list the individual jobs for each room.

Cleaning House	Self	Mate	Child 1	Child 2
Dusting				
Vacuuming				
Polishing furniture				
Mopping floors				
Cleaning windows				
Making beds				
Straightening up				
Cleaning sinks, tubs, countertops, toilets				

Laundry	Self	Mate	Child 1	Child 2
Changing linens				
Doing the wash				
Folding clothes				
Putting clothes away				
Ironing				
Sewing or mending				

Childcare	Self	Mate
Dressing		
Chauffeuring		
Helping with homework		
Reading to them		
Playing with them		
Putting them to bed		
Shopping for them		
Attending school meetings		

Home Maintenance	Self	Mate	Child 1	Child 2
Repairs				
Painting				
Gardening				
Mowing				

Money Matters	Self	Mate	Child 1	Child 2
Paying the bills				
Keeping records				
Balancing the checkbook				
Banking				

Pet Care	Self	Mate	Child 1	Child 2
Shopping for food				
Feeding them				
Cleaning up				
Bathing				
Trips to vet				
Exercising them				

SO IT'S NOT PERFECT

I know that many women complain that their husbands don't do enough chores in the home. I heard one woman say to another recently, "Do you know what a man's idea of helping with the housework is?" Her friend responded with a no. "Lifting his feet up so you can vacuum under them."

Whenever I hear a woman complain that her mate won't help with the chores, I'm reminded of a cartoon I saw many years ago. It was divided into four frames. In the first frame, the husband is cooking, and the wife, with an angry look, says, "If you don't watch carefully, you'll burn the food." In the second frame, he's cleaning the dishes, and she yells, "You forgot to scrub the pan. I can still see some food on it!" In the third frame, he's doing the laundry, and she screams, "Don't forget the bleach." In the last frame, the woman is alone and confused as she asks, "I wonder why John hates doing housework?"

Many times a husband's first attempt at helping around the house with chores is clumsy. If you begin by pointing out the inadequate job he's done changing the baby's diaper, for example, or how he cleaned up the dishes incorrectly, he'll be very reluctant to pitch in again. Even if it seems obvious to you that there is a better way to do something, resist the urge to show your mate the "right" way. Many wise women have taught themselves to become nearsighted and not expect perfection when they delegate responsibilities. Unless there is potential danger that real damage will be done if your mate is not corrected, tell yourself, "I'm not going to offer advice unless I'm asked for it."

For example, one mother I know is the president of her children's PTA. She had to be away from home last year for three days on PTA business. When she returned home, she learned from her ten-year-old son and her eight-year-old daughter that their father had added bleach to the dark clothes when he did the laundry, and all the clothes had faded. Theresa managed to swallow her criticism and not say anything. After all, she had had a wonderful time and enjoyed her respite from the house and kids. Why jeopardize her chances to go away for a few days in the future by pointing out her husband's error and making him defensive? she reasoned. Another woman I know said she had to bite her tongue when she and her husband first started sharing the chores. "It took Mike forever just to make the beds," Lana said. "I could have made them in half the time, but I knew if I wanted him to continue, I'd better reinforce what he did and not criticize how long it took. Now he's really good at it. It just took some time."

Some men may resist doing housework in very subtle ways. For instance, on a subconscious level they seem to understand that if they act helpless or pretend they don't know how to do something the "right" way, you'll automatically take over. Of course, women have been known to engage in this kind of behavior, too. One of my students delighted the class when she told this story about her grandmother. "My grandmother was a 'career woman' at the turn of the century who didn't marry until she was in her mid-thirties," said Sandra. "The first time she did my grandfather's laundry, she ironed all of his pants so that the crease, instead of being in the center of the pant leg, was pressed in along the side seams. When my grandfather took out a pair of pants and saw the way they had been ironed, he told my grandmother that he appreciated her efforts, but he didn't want her to work so hard. 'I'll do my own laundry from now on,' he said.

"As my mother always said, my grandmother was no dummy. She had very cleverly arranged it so that she didn't have to do her husband's laundry anymore," Sandra concluded.

Women who insist on giving directions and controlling their husband's housecleaning methods will usually end up responsible for the entire home. When their mate doesn't meet their standards, they "kill" themselves trying to do it all alone. The worst part is that a man who is married to this type of woman may have a tough time being romantic because he begins to see her as his mother rather than his lover.

I know it can be very upsetting to watch someone do a job that you know you could do faster and better, but remember, "practice makes perfect" (or at least better), and the only way your mate will practice is if he's allowed to feel good about his efforts. Julie remembered this when her husband agreed to go to the supermarket for the first time. "It was so hard not to criticize when I saw the bill," she confided to the class. "I'm a bargain hunter and always use coupons to save money. My husband was so proud of himself because he had found everything on the list. But he had spent a third more than I would have spent. If it weren't for what I learned in this class, I would have told him that he paid too much. But I shut my mouth, gave him a hug, and told him I was a very lucky woman to have such a helpful husband."

Charlotte's husband had stopped doing any chores years ago because whatever he did was met with ridicule and criticism. As Charlotte took a good look at her need to be in control, she began to relax a little. She learned to allow for individual differences and realized that her way was not necessarily the "right" or "only" way. With some encouragement and praise, her husband began to take on more responsibility, and Charlotte's load lifted. She learned to "lighten up" and put more effort into her husband and kids than she did into her housecleaning.

CHILDREN ARE PLAYERS, TOO

We all know how important it is for children to have good self-esteem. But the fact is, you can't *give* children self-esteem. Children *build* self-esteem by being recognized as productive members of society, starting with the family. To gain self-esteem, children must feel useful and needed. All children are eager to help and, if encouraged at an early age, will be willing helpers until the day they strike out on their own. Expect your children to help at home, and when they do, reward them lavishly with messages like "Because of you my life is so much easier" and "I don't know what I'd do without you."

Children should learn at an early age that everyone living in the home is expected to keep it comfortable and attractive, each according to his or her ability. Even a two-year-old can be helpful and made to feel important. He can carry unbreakable items such as napkins, silverware, and salt and pepper to and from the dinner table, and he can also carry his own dinner plate. He can help you dust, push a sweeper, or wipe off the table with a damp sponge. The following is a sample of some of the jobs a child is capable of doing, depending on his age.

A Three-to-Four-Year-Old Can:

- Get dressed
- Help you dust
- Put toys away
- Empty trash in small wastebaskets
- Hang up his own coat on a small hook
- Carry a light grocery bag

A Five-to-Six-Year-Old Can:

- Make his bed
- Set and clear the table

- Help pack her lunch
- Wash fruits and vegetables
- Help put some of the groceries away
- Help feed the pet
- Water the plants

A Seven-to-Eleven-Year-Old Can:

- Help prepare meals
- Clean up her own room
- Help sort and fold the wash
- Take out the trash
- Sweep the floor
- Mop the floor
- Pack his own lunch
- Rake the leaves

Children Twelve Years Old and Older Can:

- Baby-sit younger siblings
- Wash windows
- Run errands
- Mow the lawn
- Trim hedges
- Plan and prepare meals
- Iron
- Wax the floor
- Load and unload the dishwasher

When they see this list, many women in my class are shocked to learn how capable kids really are and what they can accomplish at an early age. Even after they're convinced that their kids are capable of helping, they often express doubt about getting their children to cooperate. Mimi was a typical example. She

sounded agitated when she said, "You don't understand. I can't go home tonight and announce to my
two kids that from now on they are going to do the
following chores. I can't even get them to make their
beds." Oh, yes, she could!

THE FAMILY CHALK TALK

Once you have recruited your husband as a key member of the "home team," it's time to include the children in your game plan. Call a family meeting and
present your new plan to your children. Explain
which jobs you and your mate will be responsible for
and then show the children a list of jobs they can do.
Listen to their complaints and suggestions and then
let them choose from a variety of options, rather than
making the decisions for them. If you give them a
voice, they will feel like an important part of the team
and will be far more likely to live up to their responsibilities. Be sure to make a list of the jobs they agree
to and give them copies to keep.

Tell the children that assignments will be rotated
every once in a while to adjust for changing interests,
individual likes and dislikes, and the needs of the
household. When they change jobs, children tend to
become less bored and have a chance to learn more.

PRACTICE MAKES PERFECT (ALMOST)

Everyone seems to understand the importance of
practice when learning to play a musical instrument
or participating in a sport. Many women, however,
have a difficult time realizing that it also takes prac-

tice to become skilled at making beds, washing dishes, vacuuming, or doing other household chores. If you take over a chore for a child because you know you can do it better and faster, then the child never gets the chance to practice. If you are the type of parent who says, "I'll pour the milk because you'll spill it," "I'll make the bed because you'll do a sloppy job," or "I'll clean your room because it will take you too long," then you aren't giving your child enough practice doing things for himself. It's important to realize that when a young child gives you *help*, it's probably going to take more time to complete the job than if you were to do it yourself. Instead of getting frantic about what needs to be done *today*, try to take a long-range view, keeping in mind the big picture. Children between the ages of two and four seem to have the greatest interest in helping. This is an ideal time to encourage them. Don't make the mistake of pushing your children aside or belittling their efforts because they are more trouble than help. Being patient and understanding while your child is still young will bring much better results than waiting until the child is older and then suddenly trying to force him to do chores. If children aren't encouraged when they are interested, they can't be expected to want to help when they are older. You must also be careful not to use work as a form of punishment. If Mary is told, "You've been a bad girl. As punishment, you can clean up the mess in the basement and you are not allowed to go outside until it's all done," you can't expect Mary to think of work as a positive thing.

WHEN IN DOUBT, PRAISE

Praise is one of the most valuable teaching tools and motivators that you can use as a parent. If you have a child who has been difficult to handle and hasn't helped with the chores, I'd like you to try this experiment. For one entire day, don't criticize the child in any way. Instead, seize every opportunity to praise her. Observe the child closely and praise her lavishly for any little thing she does, such as carrying her plate from the table to the kitchen sink. You can say something like "Oh, Chelsea, thanks so much for pitching in. I really appreciate it." If your child helps you carry a package, be sure to say, "What would I do without you? You are such a great help to me." You'll find that as your child's behavior is noticed and praised, she will become more and more helpful.

Parents who have adopted this technique after learning about it in class have had wonderful results. Jan went home from class determined that the next day she was going to praise her son for his behavior, rather than criticize him. However, when he left his bike out on the lawn instead of putting it in the garage, she wondered how she could make a positive statement about his forgetfulness. After thinking it over, she said, "You know, Eddy, you are always so good about putting your bike away. I wonder what happened today?"

"It's just amazing how easy it is to change a child's response with a little praise," Jan told the class. "After my comment, Eddy ran outside and put his bike away immediately."

Connie admitted she was in the habit of criticizing

her daughter for not making her bed correctly. After our class discussion, she decided to try another way. "This time," Connie said, "I looked my daughter straight in the eye and told her that every day she is learning to make her bed better and better."

"She just beamed, and after that she began tucking in the corners," Connie said, obviously pleased.

Norma's son left a toy on the stairs. Instead of her usual yelling, Norma simply said, "You always remember to pick up your toys and put them in the toy chest. I think there's something on the stairs that you forgot." Her son quickly grabbed the toy and put it in the box.

Phil shared with his class that he never acknowledged it when his son took out the trash. This time he noticed. "I just said, 'Hey. Thanks for taking out the trash.' My son kind of rolled his eyes, and I could tell he was pleased because he smiled and said, 'What's gotten into you?' "

Often, the best ideas are the simplest. If you stop and think about it, nobody likes to be criticized. Why should we, as parents, treat our children any differently than we would like to be treated? Treating your children with respect, encouraging them to learn and improve, and helping them feel worthwhile as they practice new skills will yield results that are sure to astound you. Try it. You'll like it.

WHAT'S IN IT FOR ME?

I recall an episode of *The Cosby Show* where the youngest daughter, Rudy, refused to eat her brussels sprouts. After much coaxing and pleading Cosby became annoyed. He tells Rudy that she's not going to get up from the table unless she eats her brussels sprouts, and he doesn't care if it takes all night and all the next day. He and his wife go upstairs and get ready for an evening out. Rudy is still sitting at the dinner table with the sprouts on her plate. After a while her older sister comes in with her friends. They rearrange the furniture and roll up the rug. When Rudy asks what they are doing, her sister tells her they are going to dance. Rudy asks if she can dance, too, and her sister says, "You can if you eat your brussels sprouts." She had hardly finished the sentence before Rudy had eaten all of her brussels sprouts.

You're probably wondering why I told you this story. The point is, we all want to know what's in it for us if we do what someone else wants us to do. For Rudy, the reward of getting up from the table wasn't enough for her to endure the torture of eating the brussels sprouts, but the chance to dance with her sister and her friends was.

Like Rudy, we all want some return for our effort. Nobody does anything for nothing. Often, the reward for a job well done is monetary, but many studies have shown that people will do more for praise than they'll do for a paycheck. Attention, praise, appreciation, acceptance, and admiration are all motivators for us to do something that pleases another person.

For example, my husband makes breakfast every Saturday morning, but that hasn't always been the case. For years, I made breakfast for the family every day. One Mother's Day, Steve brought me breakfast in bed as a special treat. He had made French toast and had added some cinnamon and other secret ingredients to the batter. It was the best French toast I had ever eaten! Not only did I tell Steve how much I liked it, everyone I spoke to got to hear about Steve's

French toast. Now French toast is served every Saturday at our house—by my husband. Although I hadn't planned on having Steve take over cooking breakfast on Saturdays, there is no doubt in my mind that it is now his responsibility because of all the praise he received the first time he did it.

Sometimes, when I tell this story, one of the women in class will share her own positive-reinforcement story. For example, Carla explained why her husband now does all the grocery shopping. "A few years ago I was sick in bed with the flu for two weeks, and my husband had to do all the shopping. I had never paid attention to the expiration date that appears on most food labels, but my husband did. When he came home, he went through almost everything he had purchased, explaining how he had selected the freshest bread, the most recently packaged meat and milk, and so on. Well, I made such a big deal about how much better he was at shopping than I was that he volunteered to take on that responsibility, saying that he actually enjoyed it."

Here are some little ways you can show your husband your appreciation for a job well done:

- Blow him a kiss when he's changing the baby's diaper.
- Hug him after he's put the toddler in the high chair.
- Whisper in his ear that you want to make love after the chores are done.
- Tell him how sexy he looks and feel his muscles when he's vacuuming.
- Hide a love note in the bucket he'll use to wash the car.
- Put a small gift in the grass catcher of the lawn mower.

Children need rewards, too. If you want to keep their cooperation and goodwill, you have to let them know their efforts are appreciated. Always be generous in rewarding good behavior. It's so much easier than having to deal with bad behavior.

The following are some ways you can reward your children:

- An eight-year-old might love an extra bedtime story because he straightened up the family room.
- A twelve-year-old might enjoy staying up an extra hour to play a family game because all the chores are finished.
- A teenager may welcome having a party once the garage is cleaned.

A great way to reward the whole family for doing the heavy "spring" cleaning is to have a garage sale and put whatever money you make toward a family vacation. Finally, make a list of weekend trips that the whole family can take as a reward for completing big projects or a "work" weekend. When you reward the team with a family recreational activity, you bond the family more closely together.

OUTSIDE HELP

Most people agree that it is very pleasant to have a clean and orderly home. Sometimes, however, it just isn't possible to achieve this with your immediate family, and you need outside help. With the busy schedules prevalent in so many families today, hiring outside help is the only way to have any leisure time. In addition, having outside help can reduce stress and end arguments about the endless burden of housework.

It's not necessary to hire live-in domestic help to enjoy the benefits of outside help. Except for cooking meals, most of the household chores can be done by part-time independent people. It's up to you to decide how many hours you can afford and exactly what you want them to do.

The following suggestions come from some of my students who are now managing their homes with less stress and more ease.

- Lola hired a high school girl to come in on Saturdays. "I save up about fifteen things for her to do," said Lola. "The way I look at it, that's fifteen fewer things I need to do."
- Jacob used to dread Saturdays because of all the yard work, so he hired a high school boy to mow the lawn and take care of the yard. "It's great," says John. "Now I can relax, watch some sports, and spend time with my kids without collapsing from exhaustion."
- Betty hired her neighbor's live-in to work one day a week. "She was looking for extra income, so I hired her one day a week," said Betty. "It's given me eight extra hours a week that I enjoy to the hilt."
- Mona found a retired man in her neighborhood to take the kids to and from their extracurricular activities. "He's thrilled to be needed, and it's a great time-saver," says Mona.
- Nadine found a seamstress to mend and alter her children's clothes. "She actually pays for herself," Nadine said. "The clothes I used to throw away are now fixed and reused. She's even redone some of

my older dresses to give them a more updated look."

- Liza said, "With three preschoolers, my laundry never ends. I hired a high school girl to come in twice a week just to do laundry. She washes, dries, folds, irons, and puts away the clothes. I don't know how I managed before."

- Stuart and his wife advertised at the local college for a mother's helper. In exchange for room and board, they found a college student to share in the chores and help out with the kids. "My wife is very happy with the arrangement, and so am I. After all, I get the benefit," said Stuart.

- Connie is thrilled now that the boy next door walks the dog three times a day. "It was always a hassle to decide who walks the dog. My neighbor's son loves his new job, and my husband and I love the extra time. When our children are a little older, they can take over. But for now the problem is solved."

There is nothing as precious as your time. Once it is gone, it can never be regained. Stop and think a minute about what you could do with some extra time. Perhaps you'd exercise more, read a novel, have a better sex life, or simply feel less stressed. Don't give up the possibility of having more time in your life by assuming that you cannot afford outside help. With a little creativity, you may be able to find a way to fit it into your budget. The following are a few of the ways some of my students have found to generate the money for outside help:

- Skip was in the habit of eating lunch out every day of the week. Now he goes out two days and brings his lunch the other three. *Savings: $96 a month*

- Celeste used to let her three children go to the movies every week and gave them money to buy treats. Now they go to the movies once a month and rent videos and make popcorn at home the rest of the time. *Savings: $70 a month*
- Joanne decided to buy fewer clothes for herself and less expensive clothes for her children. *Savings: $100 a month*
- Richelle uses coupons and shops the supermarket specials to save money on the grocery bill. *Savings: $60 a month*
- Laurie gave up her manicures and started doing her nails herself. *Savings: $60 a month*
- Charlie loved to play golf, but it was very expensive to play on the better golf courses every weekend. Now he plays at less expensive courses or takes a starting time late in the day, when fees are lower. *Savings: $150 a month*
- Al and Shannon ate dinner out three or four nights a week. Now they eat out once a week and prepare simple, quick meals the other times. *Savings: $180 a month.*

No matter how tight your budget, there are probably some ways you can cut corners in order to hire extra help. It may mean some sacrifices, but you'll be getting something priceless instead—time for yourself, your mate, and your children.

ASSIGNMENT #8

Becoming a Better Parent

1. Call a family meeting and divide up the housework among all the members of the family.

2. Make a list of who is responsible for each chore and post it for everyone to see.
3. Give your children time to get used to the new routine. No matter what they do, be very positive and ignore what they aren't doing for a while. Use positive reinforcement, saying things like:

- I really appreciate everything you remembered to do on that list.
- Thanks so much for setting the table. It really is such a help.
- Thanks for making your bed.
- I really love the way you folded the wash.
4. In the beginning, help your children remember to do their chores by leaving a note on the refrigerator or the counter.

Becoming a Better Partner

1. Make a date with your mate to discuss the division of chores. Let your partner know what he or she will gain from taking on his or her fair share.
2. Praise your mate frequently and let him or her know how much you appreciate his help.
3. Discuss the possibility of hiring outside help. Talk about what you would do with the extra time and how it can fit into your budget.
4. To show your mate that work can be fun, schedule a supermarket race. Divide the list of groceries in half and see who can buy everything on the list and get through the checkout stand first. The winner gets to pick whatever he or she wants as a prize. Anything goes!

Nine

*

IT'S WHAT YOU SAY
AND HOW YOU SAY IT

COMMUNICATION IS AN ACQUIRED SKILL

If I want to know how good a couple's sex life is, all I have to ask them is how well they communicate. I know that a man and a woman who spend quality time talking to each other every day are much more likely to have a close sexual relationship than a couple whose conversation is limited to a factual exchange regarding the need to take the car in for service, the upcoming school play, or little Johnny's recital.

In the beginning of a relationship, our only goal is to find out as much as possible about the other person. We shut out the rest of the world so we can spend time alone with our lover discovering everything there is to know about each other. We create a world for lovers only, in which it doesn't matter who begins the conversation or who has more to say. All we notice is how comfortable and safe we feel as we share intimate details about ourselves that we have never shared before. Our dates are followed by phone calls that last for hours.

Years later, a typical conversation for this same couple, the very ones who could once stay up all night talking, is likely to go like this:

He comes home from work and sits down to read the newspaper. She sits next to him and says, "Talk to me."

He says: Talk to you! About what?

She says: Anything, I don't care.

He says: But I don't have anything to talk about.

She says: There must be something.

He says: Honestly. I don't have anything to say. There's nothing to talk about.

If this scenario is reminiscent of the conversations between you and your mate, then you are having a problem with communication. And, if communication has become a problem for you outside the bedroom, it's a sure bet you're having trouble in the bedroom as well.

Real communication is much more difficult than most people realize. Far too many couples and parents fail to communicate with each other or their children—not because they lack the desire, but because they don't know how. Few of us learned communication skills as children. Instead, we learned that silence is golden, children should be seen and not heard, and it is not good to wear your heart on your sleeve. These homilies, coupled with the examples set by our parents, stifled communication and taught us that self-revelation was bad. The good news is that communication skills can be learned. There are definite rules to follow for improved communication, and when put into practice they will facilitate greater understanding and cooperation between you and your mate and you and your children.

THE *I*'S HAVE IT

To increase your chances of being heard and understood, it's necessary to learn to send *I* messages instead of *you* messages. In simple terms, an *I* message is: "I feel hurt"; a *you* message is: "You hurt me."

The difference between an *I* message and a *you* message is that in the first case, you take responsibility for your feelings, decreasing the possibility that your mate will feel defensive. In the second case, you're blaming someone else for your feelings, which practically guarantees that your mate will feel attacked. It's very hard to argue with an *I* message. On the other hand, *you* messages make people defensive and back them into a corner. They tend to offend, antagonize, attack, annoy, hurt, or even outrage a person.

In the following examples, it is easy to see how the *you* messages discourage communication, while the *I* messages encourage it.

Compare: "I really get discouraged when you don't help me with the dishes. It takes so much longer to do them by myself and then I have less time to spend with you."

Versus: "*You* never help around here."

Compare: "I'm really disappointed when you're not there to greet me when I get home. I miss you all day and can't wait to have you in my arms."

Versus: "All *you* care about are the kids. *You* never pay any attention to me."

A LOVING WAY OF PRESENTING YOUR NEEDS

Imagine what it would be like to be in a relationship in which your mate did everything possible to fulfill your needs, and you did the same in return. That's how a good relationship should be, and that's how your relationship can be if you are willing to make some changes. First, you must recognize what you want, which may not be as easy as it sounds. Second, you must be able to present your needs in a way that will make your mate want to please you.

Most men and women tend to blame, criticize, ridicule, threaten, order, or call each other names when trying to explain what it is that they are unhappy about. Then they can't imagine why they don't get the response they are looking for. I think what happens when we are approached in this negative way is that we react as if it were our parents making the request. I don't know about you, but my parents never gave me an explanation when they wanted me to do something. They just told me to do it. If I dared to ask, "Why?" I was told, "Because we said so!" To tell you the truth, there were many times when I wanted to say, "Don't tell me what to do," "You can't make me," but I didn't for fear I'd never see my next birthday. I think it's likely that some of those kinds of thoughts are triggered when our mate approaches us the way our parents did.

One woman told me that her husband used to shake his finger in her face when he wanted to get a message across, just as her mother used to do when she was a child. This made her so angry that she couldn't listen to anything he had to say. Finally, she was able to make him understand how self-defeating his finger-shaking was. When he stopped shaking his finger like an angry parent, his wife started listening to what he was saying.

We need to be very careful to present our requests and needs in a way that will open communication instead of closing it. Darla was very frustrated with her husband when she enrolled in my class. She was constantly yelling at him because, as she put it, "I just can't get through that thick skull of his." When I asked her to give the class an example of a typical conversation, here's what she said:

"I've had a terrible day. The kids have been giving me a hard time, and I'm exhausted. Why can't you spend some time with them? All you do is come home, eat, watch TV, and then fall asleep. It's not fair. You're their father. How can you be so lazy and inconsiderate?"

Here's what she changed it to:

"Darling, I really need your help. Today was a very tough day. I'm exhausted. I would really like to spend some time with you later this evening, but I will never make it unless I can take a hot bath and relax for a little while. Can you get the kids calmed down and put to bed? I would really appreciate it."

Darla's new way of presenting her needs gave her a more willing partner.

Darla's husband, Floyd, gave his version in the men's class:

"Every time I come home, you tell me how tired you are. You never want to have sex anymore. You always put the kids first, and I end up with the crumbs. What do you do all day that gets you so tired? I work hard, and I'm still ready to make love.

You need to get your priorities straight."

Here's what he changed it to:

"Honey, I've noticed how tired you are recently. You've been working extremely hard and look like you could use a break. I'd really like for us to spend more time together. I need to feel close to you again. Maybe we could hire someone to come in and help or I could do more to help out. I love you and miss you."

Darla and Floyd learned how to describe in loving terms what they really wanted and needed, without attacking or blaming. They were able to share their real feelings. In return, they received the response they had hoped for.

ARE YOU LISTENING?

If the first part of communicating is sending a message, the second part of communication is receiving the message. To receive a message, you must *listen*. There is a vast difference between hearing and listening. In order to hear, you need only your ears. You can be watching television or reading the newspaper and still hear your children's laughter, pots and pans banging in the kitchen, birds singing, rain on the roof, or the stereo blasting from your teenager's room. Hearing takes no concentration, no effort, no focusing.

Listening, on the other hand, requires that your brain and your heart be involved, along with your ears. Unlike simply hearing, listening takes concentration, effort, and focusing. In order to listen effectively, you can either:

1. Eliminate distractions and stop talking, stop fidgeting, and stop thinking about other things, or
2. Postpone listening until you can do all of the above.

How many times has your mate asked, "Are you listening?" as you answered, "Sure," without putting down your magazine or turning off the TV? Have you ever been caught lying when your mate asked, "Oh, yeah? What did I just say?"

When you want to give your mate your undivided attention, the kindest, most considerate things you can say are:

- Let's ask the children to leave the room so I can concentrate on what you're saying.
- I'm going to take the phone off the hook (or turn on the answering machine) so we won't be bothered.
- Let's sit somewhere where we can be comfortable and relaxed while you tell me what's on your mind.
- Let me turn off the television so I can listen to what you want to say.
- Let's go where we can have some privacy.

The above messages immediately communicate at least one of the following:

- I really want to hear what you have to say.
- Your feelings are important to me.
- I'd like to hear your point of view.
- I'd like to comfort you.
- I care what you think.
- I value your opinion.
- You are interesting to me.

If you don't listen, really *listen*, to your partner, you may be in for an unpleasant surprise. I'll never forget how devastated Kevin, a man in his forties, was when he discovered his wife had packed up her belongings and left with the two children. She had left him a note telling him she wanted a separation. When Kevin asked for my help in getting his wife to come back, he revealed that he was shocked when he found the note.

"You must have had an inkling that she was unhappy," I said. "What did she tell you was the problem?"

"Who listened?" he responded.

It's unbelievable how many times I've asked that question and gotten the same answer.

Men aren't the only ones in a relationship who don't listen. A woman can become so involved with the children, her career, or her social commitments that she ignores her mate's attempts at communication. When that happens, she runs the risk of losing him to someone who has time to listen.

When my student Penny complained that her husband was having an affair, I asked her what her husband had said in the months before the affair began.

"I honestly don't know," she answered. "I was so involved with the kids that I didn't pay any attention to what he was saying."

Franklin's life was shattered when he learned that his wife was in love with another man. When he confronted her and demanded to know the truth, she told him, "Yes, it's true. Bruce listens to me, something you've never done. He makes me feel like I'm important and my opinions and ideas count."

THE FEELINGS BEHIND THE WORDS

Most of us never learned how to express negative feelings such as anger, fear, or sorrow. In fact, most of were taught that not only was expressing those feelings unacceptable, the feelings themselves were unacceptable. Ironically, when we stifle our negative feelings, we also stifle our positive feelings. That's why so many of us also have a difficult time feeling and expressing joy, happiness, and love. Actually, even referring to our feelings as positive or negative puts a value judgment on them that is undesirable. Our feelings are not good or bad—they just are. Labeling them interferes with communication, just as surely as lack of skill does.

To be a good listener, it is very important to try to understand what a person is feeling, rather than just listening to the words as he or she communicates with you. Expressing themselves verbally is very difficult for many people. Your mate or your children may stumble over their words or say things they really don't mean as they try to communicate with you. The expression "a heart-to-heart talk" means you not only speak from your heart, but you also listen with your heart.

There is nothing more comforting than to know another person understands what you are feeling, whether it's joy, excitement, anxiety, fear, or pain. Most of the time, when your mate or child confides in you or discloses his or her innermost feelings, all he or she needs is empathy. They do not want or expect you to solve their problems or make their feelings go away. This seems to be a very difficult concept for men, especially, to grasp. One woman I know, after a couple of failed relationships, realized that men are often overwhelmed when confronted by a woman's emotional outcry. When she remarried, she told her new husband, "Don't be frightened when I cry. Sometimes I just feel especially needy for no apparent reason. When that happens, I don't need you to solve the problem, all I need is to be held and listened to." She said he got the message, and, in five years of marriage, he has never failed to respond to her "crying jags," as she calls them, with love and understanding.

There is nothing more upsetting than confiding your feelings to the one person you love more than anyone else in the world and getting a totally insensitive response, such as:

- "You shouldn't feel that way."
- "Why do you have to be so emotional?"
- "Why do you always make a big deal out of nothing?"
- "Don't be silly. There's nothing to worry about."
- "Boy are you negative."
- "Lighten up! You have no control over what's going to happen. What will be will be."

Or, your loved one tries to make you feel better by telling you about someone else's problems: "If you think you have problems, wait till you hear what happened to Isabelle."

You'll be a better listener and more supportive if you can remember that when your mate or your children come to you with a problem, they don't want solutions. They just want love. Try to keep in mind that what they're really saying is:

"Please just listen to me. I want to share what happened or what I'm worried about. I don't really want any advice or solutions. I just want you to listen to me and to understand what I'm saying and, most of all, to care about how I'm feeling."

Even small children need their feelings validated.

"But my son, who's three, says he hates his new baby sister," Jill said, when I presented this idea in class. "If I validate his feelings, won't I be giving him permission to hate?"

"No," I answered. "You're just giving your child permission to discuss all of his feelings openly—the bad ones as well as the good ones. You're letting him know that his feelings don't scare you or shock you, and that you understand exactly how he feels."

Think how much healthier a child would be if he were told, "I know you hate your sister right now. After all, she's taking a lot of my time. Eventually, though, you'll see that you love having a sister to play with and talk to," rather than being told he "shouldn't feel that way."

As parents, we have the opportunity and the responsibility to model good communication skills for our children and validate their feelings. I'll never forget the time, many years ago, when my daughter came home from her first day in junior high school sobbing so hard that she could hardly speak. When I asked her what happened, she choked out between sobs, "All of my friends got third-period lunch except me. When I went to lunch, I didn't know anyone in the cafeteria, so I just picked a table and sat down. I didn't know that the girls who were already sitting there were all eighth-graders, and one of them gave me a dirty look and said they didn't want any puny seventh-graders sitting at their table. I didn't know what to do, so I just got up and threw away my lunch

and went to the library until lunch period was over."
As she related this to me, she was crying so hard that
she could hardly breathe. How would you have responded to this situation? Would it have been in any
of the following ways?

1. Gee, honey, I'm sorry that happened. Did you try
   to be friendly or did you just sit there like a "bump
   on a log"? Conversation is a two-way street, you
   know. Maybe you looked unfriendly.
2. You're going to have to make new friends now that
   you're in seventh grade. You can't hang on to your
   old friends forever, you know.
3. You mean that's it? The way you were carrying on,
   I thought you must have had your arms and legs
   amputated.

While it might have been tempting to evaluate the
situation for her, that wasn't what she needed. She
needed me to understand how painful it was for her
to feel so alienated and alone in a crowd. Now, if for
a moment I can stop being me, with all my years of
experience and "wisdom," and try to become, instead,
a twelve-year-old who has just felt rejection, then my
response will be more appropriate. What I actually
did was hold her in my arms and say, "Oh, sweetheart, that's awful. I'm so sorry. I'll bet you don't even
want to go back to school tomorrow." I validated her
feelings by letting her know that I understood what
she had gone through. Since she felt understood, my
daughter was able to let go of her hurt feelings and
concentrate on solving the problem herself, with no
help from me. The next day she asked a girl in one
of her classes to go to lunch with her.

Roger, a student in one of my men's classes, had an

opportunity to use this new knowledge one night shortly after he learned it. It was very late at night, and it had just begun to rain, accompanied by much thunder and lightning. His five-year-old son ran into Roger's bedroom crying, "I'm scared, Daddy." Roger said that prior to the class he probably would have sent his son back to bed and told him not to be a sissy. "Eric probably would have gone back to his room feeling bad, isolated and guilty," said Roger. "Instead, I was able to validate his feelings." Here's what Roger said to his son:

"I know that loud noise is scary. I used to be frightened of it, too. But I promise nothing will happen. I'm here, and I'll protect you. Now try to get some sleep."

Instead of feeling bad, Roger's son got the message that his feelings are okay and that his dad understands him.

When my children were young, it was easy to protect them from pain, disappointment, and frustration. The truth is, most of the time I was the one who created their pain by restricting them or punishing them, and I was the one who could take their pain away. But as they grow older, I am not the cause of their pain, and I can't fix it or make it go away. They have to do that by themselves. All I can do is be there for them so they can tell me about their pain and validate that what they're feeling is okay. It's not necessary to perform miracles. All that's required is to understand and accept their feelings.

"What about a terrible loss?" asked Janet. "What if their dog dies or a grandparent passes away? Aren't you supposed to comfort the child?"

My feeling is that suffering and grief are emotions that can help strengthen a child's character and promote his or her emotional growth. I believe it is more honest, and more comforting to your children, to cry with them and say, "I know your heart is breaking," or "I know how sad you must feel," than it is to deprive them of their grief by saying, "We'll get another dog" or "Grandma is much happier now. Don't be sad." Human emotions are the ties that bind us together in the family of man. When we deny those emotions in ourselves, or in our children, we deny our humanness and destroy our chance to connect with one another.

By validating our mate's feelings and making him or her feel understood, we maximize the opportunity for communication to take place and minimize the chances for misunderstandings, arguments, and hurt feelings. In the following examples, there are several ways in which you can respond to the same situation. One way will foster communication; the others will lead to unhappiness, hurt feelings, and conflict. Which do you think is the appropriate response?

Example #1: Your mate's father was expected at your house for Thanksgiving. At the last minute, he calls to say he can't make it. What do you say to your mate?

A. Don't worry about it. He's not worth getting upset over.
B. I'm so sorry. I know how much you were looking forward to his coming, and you must be very disappointed.
C. I never liked that man anyway.
D. That's the last time we ever invite him for Thanksgiving.

While any of the above answers may be an honest expression of *your* feelings, the correct answer is *B.* By validating your mate's feelings, you have shown your love and support.

Example #2: Your husband has just learned that he may lose his job in the next few months, and he's worried about finances. What should you say?

A. Good. Now you can concentrate on finding a better-paying job.
B. You were working too many hours. Maybe you can get a job with more reasonable hours so you can spend more time with me and the childrend.
C. Oh, my God. What are we going to do?
D. I know how worried you are and what a difficult time this must be for you. The kids and I are behind you 100 percent, and we'll cut back on spending so we don't make it more difficult for you.

The answer, of course, is *D.* While you may be scared, too, dumping your fear on your mate is not supportive at this time. There'll be plenty of opportunity to share your feelings as you discuss the problem and possible solutions in the days ahead.

Recognizing the feelings behind the words helped one of my students avoid an argument when he came home two hours later than expected one night.

"When I walked through the door, my wife was furious," Milton said.

"Where the hell have you been?" she screamed.

"Normally, I would have either ignored her or yelled back. Instead, I remembered what I had learned and said, 'Honey, I know you must have been worried and upset. You certainly deserved a phone call, but the meeting lasted so long that by the time I realized how late it was, I decided to come right home instead of waiting to use the phone, since there were three other people in line ahead of me.' "

Milton said he was shocked when his wife immediately calmed down and came over and gave him a kiss. He promised that next time he'd call, no matter what. Milton understood that underneath his wife's anger was a deeper feeling of fear. Hidden in her words, "Where the hell have you been?" was the real message, "I was so worried that something terrible had happened to you." A further blowup was prevented because his wife felt understood.

WHAT TO DO WHEN "NOTHING" IS WRONG

So far we've been concentrating on verbal communication. But what about nonverbal communication? How do you communicate with someone who slams doors, kicks cabinets, gives dirty looks, rolls their eyes, or resorts to the silent treatment as a means of communication?

You may choose to ignore the whole thing, figuring it will soon blow over. Or, you may ask, "What's wrong?" and when your mate responds, "Nothing," the conversation is over. Unfortunately, neither of these methods of dealing with nonverbal expressions of anger does anything to increase communication and intimacy, but the following method does seem to work:

First, you have to be willing to commit five minutes of your time to breaking through the barrier. You begin with the same question you usually ask:

"What's wrong?"

This time, however, when you get the usual answer—"Nothing"—you're not going to drop it. Instead, say:

"Please tell me what's wrong. I know something is bothering you."

Once again, the answer you get will probably be, "I told you. Nothing is wrong."

This is when it begins to get tough. Every bone in your body is telling you to leave well enough alone—it's not worth it! Yes, it is. Keep going. The fact that you are spending so much time and effort shows your mate that you really care.

By now you are about three minutes into this monologue. This time you say, "Please tell me what's wrong. I know you are upset. I must have done something to hurt you, but unless you tell me what it is, I'll never be able to do anything about it."

Your mate begins to weaken.

Here's your final attempt. I want you to say, "Please, please, tell me what's wrong, so I can make it up to you. You are the most important person in my life, and I love you with all my heart. Sometimes I can be so insensitive to you, and I just have to know what I did to cause you this pain."

Stick with this until you get an answer, no matter how discouraged you become. The alternative is worse. Living with a person who is angry and distant is no fun. This way, your mate will eventually cave in. It really will take only about five minutes, and it will be over, and both of you will feel better.

While we're on the subject of nonverbal communication, I want to caution you to watch your own nonverbal messages. You can send a negative message without saying a word. For example:

- Your wife is talking to you. Your eyes never leave the newspaper.
  The message you send is, "I'm not interested in what you

have to say. This newspaper is more interesting.''

- Your husband is telling a story you've heard many times before. You begin to roll your eyes.
  The message you send is, "You are so boring. Here we go again.''
- You've just made love and you are silent.
  The message you send is, "That was no big deal. Certainly not worth talking about.''
- Your mate is telling you about an incident she experienced that day, and you look at your watch.
  The message you send is, "Hurry up and finish. I have more important things to do.''

Sometimes it's not what you say, but what you don't say, that hurts.

I'M RIGHT, YOU'RE WRONG

Listening and being understood brings two people closer together, but if there is a problem due to a conflict of needs or a strong difference of opinion, then just being understood isn't going to solve the problem. The most important thing to keep in mind, however, is that you can't solve a problem until the feelings have been heard, understood, and validated.

Many couples never solve problems because they are too busy trying to prove who's right and who's wrong. Do you have any idea how much time and energy you waste trying to do this? Think about it! To prove your mate is wrong, you have to:

- Watch him every minute so you can get the evidence you need.
- Tell yourself over and over why he is wrong, so you

won't forget the point you're trying to make.
- Yell really loud so you make an impression.
- Call yourself names like "dummy" and "idiot" for staying with someone who is so wrong.
- Tell as many people as you can your point of view, because the more they side with you, the more you prove you're right.
- Bring up past wrongs or hurts to prove that there is a strong correlation between the past and present.

Investing all this time and energy in proving your mate is wrong leaves you no time or energy to come up with a solution.

When two people can't agree, it is necessary to compromise. But until you stop trying to *win*, you can't even do that. I know that compromising isn't the perfect solution—both of you will have to settle for less than what you want—but it's still better than a brilliant solution where one person wins and the other feels cheated, taken advantage of, or dominated.

Nikki and Jim both enrolled in my class and presented a problem that I have heard quite often. Nikki liked to make love at night, preceded by lots of romance. Jim liked sex in the morning, with no preparation. At the time they took my class, they had had no sexual contact in over six months, because neither one would budge. They had built a wall between them, and they had no idea how to break it down. In class they learned that quite often a man's hormone level is highest in the morning and a woman's is highest in the evening, and they were able to see that their conflict was not a matter of one person trying to dominate the other but was simply a biological difference. Eventually, they were able to compromise. Now, one week is devoted to romance in the evenings and the next week it's early morning sex.

Ginny and Neil were another couple who learned the art of compromise. Neil was very social and loved to be with other people. Ginny was more introverted and enjoyed time alone. They solved the problem when they realized they didn't have to do everything together. Neil joined a theater group, which kept him busy several nights a week, and Ginny was able to enjoy her evenings at home alone. On the weekends, Ginny was happy to attend the performances and go to the cast parties with Neil.

PROBLEM-SOLVING

I think a great relationship is built on caring, commitment, communication, and compromise. Here are some rules for reaching a compromise that have worked for me, as well as for thousands of other couples.

1. Discuss the problem you are having. Make sure you both listen and understand each other's point of view. Put yourself in each other's shoes. If someone were to ask you to explain how your mate feels about this particular situation, you should be able to give his or her point of view accurately.
2. Avoid calling each other names. You don't want to attack the other person.
3. Please don't bring in a third party to side with one of you. Instead of discussing your problem with other people, discuss it with your mate.
4. Stay in the present. Don't bring up the past. Stick to the problem you are trying to solve.
5. Each of you should contribute possible suggestions

to solve the problem. An atmosphere of give-and-take will be most beneficial. When you give each other permission to solve the problem together, the solution should work for both of you.

The following are a few examples of compromises reached by graduates of my seminars:

- I would be willing to go to two parties a month, if you agree to leave at midnight.
- I'd be willing to go away for the weekend, if you don't give me a hard time about working late a few evenings.
- I won't bother you when you watch a football game, if you'll take care of the kids and give me one day a week for myself.
- I don't mind seeing your parents, if you'll limit the visits to once a week.
- I don't mind if you go hunting with your buddies, if you'll spend a weekend alone with me.
- I don't mind if you go to sleep every night at nine o'clock, as long as one night a week is reserved for us to go out alone together.
- I don't mind making dinner five nights a week, but two nights I'd like a rest.
- I'll take a more active role with the kids at night, if you'll give me a half hour to unwind by myself.

MORE THAN WORDS CAN SAY

Touching is a powerful way to communicate with the people we love. It is the best way there is to say, "You are lovable," "You are safe," "You are not alone," or "I'm sorry." In her book *Anatomy of Love*, anthropologist Helen E. Fisher says, "Human skin is like a field of grass, each blade a nerve ending so sensitive that the slightest graze can etch into the human brain a memory of the moment."

Every human being longs to be touched. In the early stages of falling in love, there's lots of cuddling, hugging, kissing, and touching, but once the kids are born, we often forget how much touching means. The only time some couples touch is when they are having sex. Kissing, holding hands, hugs, pats, neck rubs, and other affectionate touching no longer takes place.

While sex is important to a good relationship, many studies have shown that touching is absolutely necessary to survival! For example, research has shown that premature infants who were given three 15-minute massages a day for ten days gained 47 percent more weight than premature infants who received routine care only. The infants who were massaged also scored higher on developmental tests and went home about six days earlier.

In 1951, a team of psychologists from Harvard University studied close to 400 five-year-olds. They found that the kindergartners whose parents were affectionate and cuddled them were happier, played better, and had fewer feeding and bed-wetting problems than the kids raised by colder, more reserved parents. In 1987, they did a follow-up study and found that as adults, these same people had longer, happier marriages and better relationships with close friends than those who did not have much holding and cuddling in childhood. Researchers have concluded that the more a child is touched, the more socially adjusted the child becomes as an adult.

Another study found that infants died in a clean but impersonal orphanage where they were not touched, and actually thrived in a prison nursery where mothers and other adults were allowed to hold and cuddle the infants.

Still another study showed that touch can actually enhance learning. College instructors were told to touch their students' arms during a regular conference. On the next exam, the "touched" students scored six points higher than the "untouched" students, and the ones who were touched had more respect and admiration for their teachers.

I think it's a shame that today's teachers can no longer touch their students for fear of being accused of improper behavior or being sued. So many of these little children come from homes where no one touches them, and they desperately need someone to connect with. Marva Collins, my idol in the field of education, took kids who couldn't read or write and had them reading Shakespeare by the end of the year. In her book *The Marva Collins Way*, she explains that every day she'd go up and down the aisles touching each child in some way—either stroking her hair, straightening his collar, or touching her shoulder. Collins makes the point that no one cares how much you know until they know how much you care. My son, who is now nineteen, still remembers his favorite first-grade teacher because she gave him a kiss.

Teenagers need to be touched just as much as younger children do. Just because your child no longer needs you to take care of him physically doesn't mean he doesn't need to be touched by you. It's true that teenagers can often be obnoxious and usually appear to be standoffish and independent. But I've never met a teenager yet who, underneath that cool, indifferent exterior, didn't need to know that his parents care about him. They may be "closet" huggers and they may complain loudly, but deep down they are feeling secure, because they know they are loved.

If a baby can die from lack of touch, it's easy to understand why some teens seek out someone to hold them and touch them. Many of my students who engaged in sex at a very early age explained that they came from a home where there was little or no touching. One woman said, "What I really needed was hugging and holding. Since I couldn't get that from my family, I looked for it in the opposite sex." Students who had come from homes that did a lot of touching waited until they were much older before experiencing a sexual relationship.

To be our best, we have to feel connected to other people, and one way to feel connected is through touch. The next time you are going to a party with your mate, or to a school function with your child, play this game with him or her. Say that while you are at the party or event, you must connect six times with a kiss. One time my daughter and I were going to a swim meet where I was to help out with registration, and she was competing. When I told her we had to connect six times that day, her reaction was, "Aw, Mom. That's so embarrassing." I told her that we could either have a full-blown scene, where I threw my arms around her and kissed her, or we could do it discreetly. Given the choice, she decided for "discreet." It turned out to be a great day for both of us. We had fun sneaking our pecks on the cheek and feeling close and connected.

Ironically, the more unlovably a person behaves, the more that person needs to be touched. Most often, we are confronted with unlovable behavior when our children are teenagers, but some adults can be pretty unlovable, too. When Candy was hurt and confused by her husband's mood swings, she was thinking of leaving him.

"I don't know what to do when he acts like that," she said. "He pouts and sulks over things that seem really insignificant to me."

I suggested that the next time her husband sulked, she try just holding him. "An adult who acts out like a two-year-old is probably a hurt child underneath all that anger. Try to see him as a hurt baby who needs to be loved, and treat him accordingly," I advised her.

A few weeks later, Candy reported that she had taken my advice. "It was like a miracle," she said. "When Lee started to withdraw and sulk, I just put my arms around him and talked to him softly like I would to a child. I said things like, 'It's all right,' 'Poor baby,' and 'I'm sorry you're hurting so much,' and he quieted down immediately. Later he apologized and thanked me for being so understanding."

Many people have what I call "skin hunger," but if you are in a relationship, this shouldn't be the case. For everyone's physical and emotional well-being, begin a "touch" program in your home today. Make it a point to hug each other at least once a day for twenty seconds. While this may sound like a short time, it isn't. By embracing for twenty seconds, you'll let go of your defenses and really connect with each other. You'll be able to relax and feel the love as it flows between you, and you will feel at peace and gain strength from each other.

TAKE TIME TO COMMUNICATE

Most women, whether they work outside of the home or not, have a great need to talk with their mate every day, and they *will* communicate—if not through conversation, then through conflict. The dilemma is that most men have a great need for solitude when they first come home from work. The answer to the dilemma is for each partner to appreciate the other's needs. She gives him time to be by himself, and he gives her thirty minutes of his undivided attention each day.

You can't expect to achieve intimacy in your relationship unless you communicate on a daily basis. I recommend that you find a time and a place where you not be interrupted or distracted in any way, and spend thirty minutes talking together every day. In case you've read this too quickly, I want to emphasize that I didn't say I recommend talking together for thirty minutes once in a while, or once a week, I said every day! During these thirty minutes there has to be a dialogue, not a monologue. Each of you is to participate in that time period, with each of you taking fifteen minutes to share the events of the day, as well as your thoughts and feelings.

Lacey said that after they took my class, she and her husband, David, made a joint decision to do this homework assignment faithfully. They hired a babysitter to come in at eight o'clock every evening to watch the children and help clean up the dishes, while they go for a thirty-minute walk. "Holding hands and talking sounds like such an insignificant thing to do, but it's brought us so close together," Lacey said.

Anita and her husband get in their hot tub for a half hour every night and talk. "The only distractions are the stars, and the water helps us relax and focus on each other," Anita said.

Dwight and Cora reported that after the kids go to bed, they turn off the TV, put some soft music on the stereo, have a drink, and talk.

Alex and Ivy were able to arrange their schedules so that they could have breakfast at a neighborhood coffee shop every morning. "To tell you the truth, we take an hour each day," said Alex. "When Ellen first gave me this assignment, I really wondered what we could find to talk about for thirty minutes, but when there's only the two of you, you have plenty to discuss."

ASSIGNMENT #9

Becoming a Better Parent

1. Take time out every day to listen to each of your children individually. Let them know that whatever they are feeling is perfectly all right.
2. Teach your children the words they need to express their feelings.

Feeling Bad	Feeling Good
I feel angry	I feel happy
I feel sad	I feel proud
I feel sorry	I feel excited
I feel mad	I feel good
I feel worried	I feel glad

3. Pay attention to your children's nonverbal clues. Encourage them to discuss what's troubling them.
4. If your children are old enough, try to get them involved in solving a problem that you're having with them.

5. Make it a habit to hug your children every day. Kiss them, hug them, cuddle with them, stroke them—touch them as much as possible.

Becoming a Better Partner

1. Begin really listening to your mate. If you're too busy to listen, make an appointment to talk later.
2. Validate your mate's feelings. Let him or her know you understand the feeling behind the words.
3. Substitute *I* messages for *you* messages whenever possible.
4. Present your needs in a loving way.
5. The next time your mate refuses to verbalize what's bothering him (or her), be persistent in encouraging him to open up.
6. Sit down and discuss a problem. Decide on a compromise together.
7. Give your mate a twenty-second hug every day this week.
8. Spend thirty minutes every day communicating with your mate with no distractions or interruptions.

Ten

✳

EVERYONE DESERVES
TO FEEL GOOD

HAPPY THOUGHTS

Years ago, Norman Vincent Peale wrote his book *The Power of Positive Thinking.* In it he revealed his revolutionary theory that our thoughts can influence the events of our lives. At the time, the scientific community scoffed at the notion that our thoughts and our reality were intertwined. Now there is scientific evidence that Dr. Peale's theory was accurate. Scientists today know that when our attitude is positive, our bodies release chemicals that make us feel good and, they believe, protect us from illness. Having a good attitude is the key to having a good life, and your attitude is something you can control.

You've all seen the principle of positive thinking in action: A man or woman who's always ready with a smile or a laugh, even in the face of extreme adversity, or the man or woman who seems to walk around under a dark cloud, even though it appears that he or she has everything good in life. The difference between them is not what they've experienced in life;

it's how they've reacted to what they've experienced. What we think, and how we translate our thoughts into an internal dialogue (what we think about what happens to us), causes us to feel a certain way. In other words, a negative thought can make us feel bad, while a positive thought can make us feel good. It's not the situation that causes us to feel good or bad, it's how we interpret the situation that determines how we feel. For example:

- Two people are forced, by circumstances, to pull up roots and move to a new area. One thinks, I will miss my friends so much. I don't think I can stand to be so far away. This person feels *unhappy*. The other thinks, How exciting this is. I've always wanted to live in a different location. Now I can explore new things and discover new places to enjoy. This person feels *happy*.
- Two men are fired from their jobs. One man thinks, Thank goodness. I hated this job, but I never would have had the guts to leave on my own. Now I can get a job I like better. This man feels *happy*. The other man thinks, Oh, no. I'm never going to find another job. There are probably thousands of people who are more qualified than I am. This man feels *unhappy*.
- Two women watch as the last of their children leaves home to be on her own. One woman thinks, This is such a wonderful time in my child's life, and ours, too. Now my husband and I will have the entire house to ourselves. She's *happy*. The other woman thinks, I have nothing to live for now. Being a mother was my whole life. Now I feel useless. No one needs me anymore. She's *unhappy*.
- Two women arrive home too late to prepare dinner.

One thinks, Oh, good. Now I have an excuse to go out for dinner. She's *happy*. The other thinks, I should have gotten home earlier. Everyone's depending on me for dinner. If I don't cook, everyone will be upset. She's *unhappy*.

• Two men have sons who've just gotten their driver's licenses. One thinks, Now he can help with the errands. It will be great to have an extra driver in the house. He feels *happy*. The other father thinks, He's too young to drive. I'm afraid he'll get into an accident. He's *unhappy*.

Do you see how, given the same situation, one person will find the positive aspects and another will focus on the negative? If you tend to be a negative person, you're probably thinking about now, Well, I can't help it. That's just the way I am. Maybe so. But chances are, you weren't born that way. You learned to be negative. Later in this chapter you'll see how many parents unwittingly teach their children to think negatively about themselves and, consequently, the world around them. The good news is that if we can learn to be negative, we can also learn to be positive.

People with a positive attitude seem to have the ability to keep things in perspective. They see individual events in the context of the big picture, rather than narrowly focusing on the current situation. One of my favorite stories is about a little boy who demonstrated this ability to see the big picture one day when he was four years old. His nursery-school teacher had broken her glasses on her way to work and came into the classroom without them. The children noticed right away that "Mrs. Elsie" wasn't wearing her glasses, as she usually did. Many of the children had opinions and comments about her lack of eyewear. One child said, "Mrs. Elsie, I like you better with your glasses on." Another child said, "Mrs. Elsie, I like you better without your glasses." One by one, the children offered their opinions. Better, worse . . . better, worse. Finally, Aaron spoke up. "Mrs. Elsie," he said solemnly, "I like you just the same with or without your glasses." This wise child knew that nothing about his beloved teacher had changed. She was the same wonderful person she'd always been—with or without her glasses.

People who are positive thinkers are happier people, and people who are happy make the people around them happier. So, to be the best parent and the best partner, you have to be a happy person yourself. Don't misunderstand. I'm not suggesting that you deny reality. If something bothers you or makes you unhappy, you need to acknowledge it, at least to yourself. By denying a problem, you only make it worse. It's like leaving a splinter imbedded in your finger. If left to fester, the wound becomes inflamed and eventually becomes infected. Remove the splinter promptly, and it only hurts for a little while. So, when a problem occurs, deal with it. Don't leave it alone to fester. Part of your "problem-solving" self-talk can be an assessment of the situation. I love the wisdom of the Serenity Prayer:

"God, grant me the serenity to accept the things I cannot change, courage to change the things I can, and the wisdom to know the difference."

If the problem you are experiencing is something you can take care of, then take care of it. If it's not (i.e., not *your* problem), then let it go. And be honest enough to acknowledge when something is your problem and when it is not.

It is definitely possible to change from a negative-thinking person to a positive-thinking person, but it takes a strong desire and a commitment to do what's necessary. Wanting to be a positive, happy person is not enough. You have to monitor your inner dialogue, listen to what you are saying to yourself, and learn, word for word, what to say to yourself instead. You have to practice every day until positive thinking becomes as natural to you as negative thinking is now. Your mind is like a computer. It can do only what you program it to do—garbage in, garbage out (GIGO). To become a happier person, you must replace the garbage, your old "negative" programming, with a brand-new "positive" program. Like all big jobs, changing how you think can be accomplished most easily by taking it one step at a time. With my help, you'll start at Level 1 and, with perseverance, you'll eventually arrive at Level 4.

Level 1: Unconscious Negative Thoughts

At this level, you have no idea that there is an internal dialogue going on, and that most of what you say to yourself is negative. You only know that most of the time you are unhappy and depressed.

Level 2: Conscious Negative Thoughts

At this level, you are now aware that you are talking to yourself. As you listen, you realize that almost everything you say to yourself is negative. You now understand that your depression or unhappiness is a direct result of your thoughts.

Level 3: Conscious Positive Thoughts

At this level, you are able to replace the old negative thought with a brand-new positive one. It feels a little awkward in the beginning, and you aren't sure you even believe the new positive thought, but you are much happier than you've been. You realize you have the power to change your thoughts.

Level 4: Unconscious Positive Thoughts

This is the highest level. At this level, you no longer have to monitor what you say to yourself. Most of what you are saying is positive. You feel good about yourself, about life, about the people who surround you, and about what you do.

STARTING OVER

What follows is a step-by-step procedure to get from Level 1 to Level 4. It sounds simple, and it is. But it's not easy. It takes hard work and commitment. Just keep in mind that the payoff is a happier you, and a happier family. And it's guaranteed to work! If you've spent years wishing life were easier, or if you've spent a lot of money on therapy that didn't make a lasting difference on your overall sense of well-being, it's time to try something different. You can be happy if you'll just follow these steps.

Step 1: The next time you feel unhappy or depressed, try to identify the negative thoughts you had just prior to feeling that way.

Step 2: Ask yourself these two questions:
  1. Do these thoughts make me happy?
  2. Are these thoughts destructive or supportive?
Step 3: Replace one negative thought at a time with a positive thought.
Step 4: Ask yourself these two questions about your new thought.
  1. Is this a happier thought?
  2. Is it supportive?

If you can answer yes to both questions, you've done a great job. The more you practice, the faster you'll get at replacing the old negative thought with a new and more positive one. Remember, you can't think two thoughts at the same time. Since you are the creator of your thoughts, you can choose to ignore the negative thought and pay attention to its replacement—which makes you feel better. Let's see how this works.

- You're late for a parent conference with your child's teacher.
  Your first, negative thoughts: I blew it! What an idiot I am. This will reflect poorly on my child.
  Your positive replacement thoughts: I didn't blow anything, and I'm not an idiot. The teacher will understand that I was unavoidably delayed. What I do has nothing to do with my child's grade.
- You get up in the morning and drag yourself into the shower.
  Your first, negative thoughts: I can hardly open my eyes. I don't want to go to work today.
  Your positive replacement thoughts: I'm lucky to be alive and have this wonderful day ahead of me. I

can't wait to go to work and do the best job possible.
- You've been on a diet and done well for one week. Now you just couldn't resist that candy bar.
  Your first, negative thoughts: I'll never lose weight. I'll always be fat. I have no willpower.
  Your positive replacement thoughts: Big deal. One candy bar against seven days of dieting. I've done a great job so far. So I slipped. There's always tomorrow. I have a great deal of willpower.
- You can't seem to fall asleep.
  Your first, negative thoughts: I'll never get to sleep. I'll be so tired I won't be able to see straight tomorrow. This is really boring, lying here waiting to sleep.
  Your positive replacement thoughts: Eventually, I'll be tired enough and will go to sleep. If I don't, I'll make up for lost sleep tomorrow night. I'll be just as rested if I lie here quietly. I may as well enjoy myself and start that book I've been wanting to read.

Begin now to practice these steps to move from a negative, unhappy person to one who is happy, confident, and positive. Use discipline to monitor your self-talk constantly until you have reached Level 4, the point at which you have become a person who automatically thinks positively. Don't do to your children what may have been done to you! Your children are your chance to be a better parent than yours were. Your children are your best chance to make this a better world. For your children's sakes, become a positive person, so you can give them more positive messages than you received.

THE POWER OF WORDS

In all my years of teaching, I've never met a parent who consciously wanted to destroy his or her child's self-esteem. Yet without realizing it, that's exactly what many parents have done. Over the years, I've made it a point to ask the parents in my classes how often they thought they gave a negative message to their child. Based on the hundreds I interviewed, the average seemed to be about ten negative messages a day. That means that by the time a child reaches the age of eighteen, he's heard over 65,000 negative messages from one or both parents. If the child was part of an extremely negative family, he could have heard as many as twenty negative messages a day, or as many as 130,000 by age eighteen.

When these same parents were asked how many positive messages they could remember hearing as children from their own parents, most could only recall hearing four or five in their entire life. Sadly, some couldn't remember hearing one single positive message from their parents when they were children. This indicates that most children hear only four or five positive messages, contrasted with 65,000 or more negatives during their entire childhood. Now can you see why so much of what you say to yourself is negative? We actually take over where our parents left off. It is no wonder that researchers have found that almost 80 percent of what we think about as adults is negative.

By talking with the men and women in my classes, I was able to compile the following negative messages that most of them heard growing up. Unfortunately, many of them will sound familiar to you as well. I want you to really listen to the negativity of every one of them so that you'll be able to stop yourself from giving these same messages to your children now that you are the parent.

NEGATIVE MESSAGES

- Can't you remember anything?
- Just who do you think you are?
- You will be the death of me yet.
- Why can't you do anything right?
- If your head wasn't attached to you, you'd lose it.
- Watch where you're going.
- You are such a spoiled brat.
- Shame on you!
- You are such a troublemaker.
- You make me so mad.
- I wish you were never born.
- Why can't you be good for a change?
- You are such an idiot.
- You are no good.
- You are so naughty.
- You are so sneaky.
- I don't know what to do with you.
- Having you was a big mistake.
- Can't you give me a break?
- Why can't you behave?
- You are such a "busybody."
- You are such bad luck.
- You are an accident waiting to happen.
- You can't be trusted.
- You can't handle anything.
- You are impossible.
- You are so stupid.
- You are driving me crazy.
- Can't you use your brain?
- Will you just shut up!

- You are such a slob.
- I want you out of my sight.
- You are such a pig.
- I don't want to see your face again.
- Are you blind?
- You have two left feet.
- You are so clumsy.
- You are hopeless.
- You are so irresponsible.
- You are a pain in the neck.
- You are getting under my skin.
- When will you ever learn?
- You make me sick.
- I can't stand you anymore.

When we were children, many of us learned from our parents that "sticks and stones can break my bones, but names can never hurt me." What a lie! Names *do* hurt—sometimes permanently. Growing up is hard. Kids take a lot of abuse from other kids, teachers, other adults, and parents. As a parent, it's your job to protect your child from cruelty and help him acquire the tools he will need to deal with the world without you. We can never underestimate the power of words. These messages may appear to be harmless, but heard often enough, these messages can destroy a child's self-esteem. Replace the negativity you learned as a child with positive thoughts and messages for your child. Remember this important point: Your brain believes what you tell it the most. When a child has heard these negative messages enough, he believes they are true. He believes he is dumb, inadequate, worthless, bad, or wrong, and his actions reflect his belief.

If you occasionally do slip and dump a negative

message on your child, apologize immediately. Hug your child and tell him you're sorry. Make it clear that you do not think he is dumb. Explain that it was his action that was dumb, if that is the case, or that something entirely unrelated to him made you act the way you did.

A SPOONFUL OF SUGAR

Children whose parents withhold positive messages when they are young are often driven by a need for parental approval as adults. Entertainers, especially, are often seeking from their audience the approval they were denied as children. When Whoopi Goldberg interviewed Ozzie Osbourne, the famous rock star, he told her that all he cared about was making his father proud of him. One day, after he had become successful, Osbourne asked his father if he was proud of him now. His father still wasn't able to give him the approval he sought. Frank Sinatra is another entertainer who was always striving to win his father's love and approval.

A child should never have to ask if his parent is proud of him or if he is loved. It is a parent's job to love and nurture his child, and that duty goes far beyond providing food, shelter, and clothing. Your goal, as a parent, should be to give positive messages to your child every single day. If you're in the habit of sending nothing but negative messages, with practice and conscientious effort, eventually you can get to the point where your positive messages replace the negative ones. The following are some positive messages that your child deserves to hear:

- I'm really proud of you.
- You always come up with such great ideas.
- You do such good work.
- You are a very special person.
- You make me so happy.
- You bring me luck.
- Your smile lights up this room.
- You are so smart.
- You are so energetic.
- Everyone loves you.
- You're always so comfortable with people.
- You make such a good impression.
- I love you just the way you are.
- I'm so happy when I'm with you.
- You can become anything you want.
- You'll go far in life.
- You are such a blessing to this family.
- You are so pretty (or handsome).
- You are so honest.
- I can always trust you.
- You always do the right thing.
- You are so much fun to be with.
- I love your sense of humor.
- You are so good at solving problems.
- You always look at the positive side.
- You have such a good memory.
- I'm so glad you're mine.
- I'm so glad you were born.
- You are such a caring person.
- You are always so well behaved.
- You can handle anything.
- You are so neat.
- You are so creative.
- You are so graceful.
- I love having you around.

- How did I get so lucky to have a child like you?
- You are unique.
- There's no one like you in the whole world.
- You are so talented.

Statements such as these make a child feel loved and help him build self-esteem. Just imagine how confident and happy a child would be who grew up in a home where, for the first eighteen years of his life, he heard sixty-five thousand positive statements and only four or five negative ones.

DARE TO DREAM

Another way that many parents destroy their child's self-confidence is by destroying the child's dreams. Without realizing what they are doing, parents will often stifle a child's ability to dream or fantasize about the future. Instead of supporting the child's fantasies and encouraging him or her by brainstorming new ideas with the child, the parent criticizes the child for dreaming and details every possible reason why his or her dreams won't work or the many obstacles that cannot be overcome. Instead of offering support and reassurance, the parent plays the devil's advocate.

A good example of this was a student named Joanne whose preschool daughter dreamed of becoming a gymnast. Joanne confessed to the class that she had discouraged Katie by explaining that gymnasts had to be very short and petite. She told Katie that since she was already taller than most of her friends, and because her parents were tall, being a gymnast was not going to be a possibility for her. Joanne also pointed out how time-consuming and dangerous this sport could be.

After taking my class, Joanne realized her error, and she immediately enrolled her daughter in gymnastics. The last I heard, although her daughter had grown another four inches, she has accumulated many ribbons and trophies and has had her dream returned to her.

Chester was another student who admitted to the class that he blew it. One night at dinner, his six-year-old son said out of a clear blue sky, "You know, I've been thinking. What I'd like to do when I grow up is become a businessman and travel all over the world." Chester, now ashamed of his reply, said, "I made him feel stupid when I insisted he define what he would do as a businessman. Then I told him how scarce jobs overseas were. Next, I pointed out how he'd probably hate being in a strange country, and to really discourage him, I talked about the possible dangers of flying, the loneliness of being on the road, and the lack of security he would have.

"I had expected Charlie to appreciate the voice of experience and my concern for his well-being, and I was surprised when he began to withdraw and quietly left the room.

"After our discussion in class, I began to really think about what you had said. I wanted so much to give my son back his dream. When I went home after class that night, I went straight to Charlie's room and asked him to move over and make room for me on his bed. I simply said, 'Remember last week when you wanted to be an international businessman? Well, I really put a damper on it, and I want you to know I'm sorry. It's a great idea. You can see the world, experience different cultures, meet interesting people, and probably make a great deal of money.' "

By giving him back his dream, Chester gave his son a positive message—one that may affect the rest of his life. Now Charlie can say to himself, "I came up with a great idea," and as a result have the confidence to continue to dream. As for Chester, he is grateful that he was able to give his son a positive message that will lead to Charlie engaging in positive "self-talk" on his own.

CATCH THEM IN THE ACT OF BEING GOOD

Children who hear positive messages instead of negative ones are more self-confident, and children who are self-confident are better behaved. Since they get praise and positive reinforcement for simply being, they have no need to behave badly to get their parents' attention. Once you have overcome your inclination to focus on the negative and to replace your negative thoughts with positive ones, you'll find it easy to focus on what your child does right and ignore what displeases you. Try to remember that if your child displeases you, it doesn't mean he is bad, naughty, or evil. It simply means that his agenda and yours are different.

To get your child to behave the way you wish, you must constantly reinforce the behavior you want. For example, suppose you want your child to play quietly or entertain herself while you talk on the phone, instead of demanding attention as soon as the phone rings. Pay close attention, and the next time you manage to have an uninterrupted phone conversation because your child happens to be watching TV or playing with her toys, reinforce the behavior. After you hang up, give your child a kiss and a hug and say enthusiastically, "Do you know what you just did?" When your child looks at you curiously and says, "No. What did I do?" tell her warmly, "You behaved so well while I was on the phone. Do you know that if I lined up ten children, they'd all act up when their mom was on the phone, but you're the best little girl a mommy can have. Thank you so much for being quiet."

I guarantee that you'll have to reinforce the behavior you want only once or twice before your child's agenda and yours will be the same. Soon, when the phone rings, your child will behave well on purpose, rather than by accident. Positive reinforcement also works to reduce squabbling between your children. In my opinion, it is the parents who reinforce the fact that brothers and sisters don't get along. Instead of saying, "You kids are always fighting. Why can't you get along?" why not comment on all the times that they *do* get along? Time and time again, my children have heard me say, "You are such good friends. Oh, sure. You argue once in a while, but you are really close." As a result, they are close.

Instead of being critical of your children, make an effort to notice everything they do that's wonderful, right, and good. If you want positive behavior to increase, start noticing at least one thing a day that you can comment on positively, no matter how small. Saying something as simple as "Do you know how much I love your smile? Every time you walk into this house, you light up the room" will produce a child who smiles readily.

Here are some other suggestions:

- What a happy voice I hear in the crib.
- How nice to see you reading that book.

- You were so quiet when Mommy was visiting with our neighbor.
- You're so good at entertaining yourself.
- You are such a good helper.

Every single day your children are being good, but most parents either don't notice or don't bother to comment. In fact, if your children are quiet while you're driving, you probably think, I'll give them three more minutes, and I'll bet they start acting up. Next time replace that negative thought with the following positive dialogue, but say it out loud: "What wonderful children I have. You're so quiet and happy looking out the window when I'm driving the car." When you begin to notice and comment on all the wonderful things your children do every day, they will respond with more positive behavior. It shouldn't require a major accomplishment for your child to be noticed and praised. Your goal should be to reward behavior you'd like to see more of on a daily basis. As you change your attitude to a more positive one, you will set in motion a chain reaction that will result in a happier, more positive child and a happier, more positive mate.

WHY WE FALL IN LOVE

Children are not the only ones who respond to positive reinforcement and praise. We all deserve to feel good, and that includes our partners. While promoting my first two books on radio and television, I was asked one question over and over again. The question was, "Why do you think men and women fall in love in the first place?" Because my answer was unexpected, I was always asked to repeat it, while the show's host, as well as the members of the audience, nodded their heads in agreement. Because I feel it's so important, and because it is the underlying theme of everything I teach and believe in, I am compelled to repeat it here.

A man falls in love because of the way he feels about himself when he's with a particular woman.

If he stops feeling good about himself when he's with her, he'll find another woman who makes him feel good about himself. That's what an affair is all about. It's not that a man is in love with the other woman. It's that he's in love with the way he feels about himself when he's with the other woman. When we talk about this in class, most men agree that once they fell in love, they felt stronger, sexier, more capable, more intelligent, and more important than they had ever felt about themselves before this special woman came into their life.

A woman falls in love for the same reason. The women I interviewed said that they felt prettier, sexier, more intelligent, more capable, and more needed when they finally met "Mr. Right" than they had ever felt about themselves before.

My classes have never been about how to become thinner, make more money, or become more beautiful, more handsome, or more intelligent. Some of the most attractive people in the world don't have a love relationship. Some of the wealthiest people are lonely. Some of the most brilliant people are alone. Being in love is really about how we feel about ourselves when we are in the presence of a person we are attracted to.

My marriage has thrived for twenty-seven years because my husband has always felt good about himself when he's with me. I have always told him how much I love him as a husband, father, and human being. By the same token, I have always felt good about myself when I'm with him. He has always reinforced how much I mean to him, how lucky my children are to have me as their mom, and how proud he is of my career. Why would either of us ever want to be with anyone else? No one could ever make us feel any better about ourselves than we already do. We have our own little "mutual admiration society."

MAKE ME FEEL GOOD

To keep love alive, you have to be able to make your partner feel good about himself or herself. Remember when you first fell in love with your mate? When your love was new, you saw all of your mate's wonderful qualities and either ignored the negative ones or didn't even notice them. That's why they say "Love is blind." Unfortunately, as time goes by and we get caught up in the business of raising our children and the daily drudgery of life, we often find ourselves focusing more on what's wrong with our mate than what's right, but this doesn't have to be the case. Just as you can change your thoughts and attitudes from negative to positive, you can change the way you see your mate. To do this, you must concentrate on looking at your mate's personality traits in the same positive way you did in the beginning. You can train yourself to do this. Then make your mate feel good by verbalizing what you love about him or her. To help yourself make this shift from negative to positive, ask yourself these questions:

- How would someone who has just fallen head over heels in love with my mate view the same personality trait that has begun to irritate me?
- If my mate had only one more day to live, what would I be focusing on?

There are two sides to every coin, and at least two ways to view every personality trait. I'll give you some examples; then it's up to you to think about your own mate in a positive light.

1. Do you view your mate as unenthusiastic? Here is a person who is calm and soothing to be with. He or she is usually levelheaded and well grounded. This person doesn't get upset at trivial matters and isn't prone to mood swings. He or she is often patient, consistent, and low-key. Statements that make this person feel good are:
   - I love the way you have such a calming effect on this family.
   - I love the fact that you are so even-tempered.
   - It's such a pleasure to be with such an easygoing person.
   - It's such a pleasure to see you so relaxed and comfortable most of the time.
2. Do you view your mate as indecisive? Here is a person who is open to all possibilities. He or she usually sees many alternatives in any given situation. This person is often flexible, open-minded, and philosophical. Statements that make this type of person feel good are:
   - I love being with someone who takes her time to make a decision and doesn't act impulsively.
   - I love being with someone who considers other people's feelings and needs along with his own.

- This family is lucky to have someone who listens to everyone's opinion and gives everyone a voice in the final decision.

3. Do you view your mate as egostistical? Here is a person who knows what he or she wants. This person is goal-oriented and usually assumes leadership roles. He or she takes on a great deal of responsibility. He or she is often independent, confident, and strong-willed. Statements that make this type of person feel good are:
   - I love the way you are always in control of a situation.
   - It's so wonderful to be with someone who feels good about herself.
   - You've taught our family to stand up for what they believe in.
   - It's great being with someone who is so positive in his approach to life.

4. Do you view your mate as disorganized? This is a person who is fun to be with. He or she has the ability to live in the present. This person is never in a hurry and will make you stop and smell the roses. He or she is often creative, spontaneous, and multifaceted. Statements that make this type of person feel good are:
   - I love the way you can do many things at the same time.
   - Our children are lucky to have someone who puts fun ahead of orderliness.
   - I love the way you don't let little things bother you.
   - I love your carefree attitude.
   - You always have such original ideas.

5. Do you view your mate as emotional? Here is a person who usually lives life in a passionate way.

He or she has a deeper level of understanding because he or she is very sensitive and intuitive. This person is often tender, compassionate, and sentimental. Statements that make this type of person feel good are:

- I love the fact that you are deeply concerned about everyone.
- I love the fact that I can tell you anything and you can feel what I feel.
- I love the fact that you emphasize our family traditions.
- I love your romantic side.

6. Do you view your mate as rigid? Here is a person you can count on. He or she is very organized and pays attention to the smallest details. This person sees things in a clear, logical way. He or she is dependable, consistent, and responsible. Statements which make this type of person feel good are:

- I love the fact that I can count on you to follow through with what you say.
- I love the fact that you'll always do a thorough job.
- I love the way you handle our children in a straightforward way. You don't give mixed messages.
- I love the fact that you have a high standard of ethics and stick to them.

7. Do you view your mate as a show-off? This is usually a person who bubbles over with enthusiasm. He or she is extroverted and is the life of the party. This person is entertaining and puts everyone at ease. He or she is often sociable, interesting, and vivacious. Statements that make this type of person feel good are:

- I love the fact that you draw attention wherever you go.
- I love the fact that life is never boring with you.
- I love the way you tell stories and captivate our children.
- I love your sense of humor.

I hope these examples have helped you to see your own mate's personality in a more positive light. By focusing on the positive side of your mate's personality, you will find it easier to make positive, loving statements. In turn, this will make your mate feel good about himself or herself once again and will keep the fire lit in your relationship. Life is too short to dwell on your mate's or your children's shortcomings. Put some blinders on and accentuate the positive.

Everyone deserves to feel good. Feel better about yourself by following the steps outlined at the beginning of the chapter. Help your children feel good about themselves by sending positive messages and supporting their dreams, and make your mate happy by verbalizing the things you love about him or her. You'll see that as you continue to notice something positive, even if it's just one little thing, you'll get an increasingly positive response. When you make someone feel good about himself or herself, he or she responds in kind.

ASSIGNMENT #10

Becoming a Better Parent

1. Pay attention to your thoughts regarding your children. If you have a negative thought, replace it with a positive one.

2. Make some "Certificates of Achievement" to award to your children each time you catch them in the act of being good.
3. For one entire week, pay attention to all their positive behavior. Praise them and give them a certificate for *any* positive act or behavior, no matter how small.
4. Start keeping a journal. Each night, before you go to bed, write down all of the positive messages you've given to your child that day. If you didn't give any praise, you owe your child double the dose the next day.

Becoming a Better Partner

1. Begin to pay attention to what you say to yourself. Whenever you have a negative thought, replace it with a positive one. Remember, it's difficult to praise someone else if you're having negative thoughts.
2. Look at your mate through new eyes. Remember what it was about your mate that you loved at the beginning. Make a list of all the wonderful traits you see.
3. Commit to making your mate feel good about himself or herself this week. Praise your mate's personality traits and let him or her know you love him or her as a parent, lover, and human being.
4. Whenever possible, praise your mate in front of other people.

CONCLUSION

I believe, as parents, you have certain rights, which, when enforced, will help you keep the fires lit and prevent you from going crazy.

A PARENT'S BILL OF RIGHTS

You have the right:

- To have a life that is separate from your children
- To take time for yourself in order to renew your energy
- To have adult relationships that exclude children
- To have privacy when needed
- To take an evening, a weekend, and a one-week vacation as lovers
- To pursue your own goals and dreams
- To have your children respect your property

In addition, I believe that your children have certain rights, which, when granted, will help them to grow up as secure, self-confident adults.

A CHILD'S BILL OF RIGHTS

Your children have the right:

- To be treated with respect
- To be raised in a loving, safe home
- To have their wishes considered
- To have a life separate from the family
- To have privacy when needed
- To have their property respected
- To do nothing but daydream occasionally
- To learn from their own mistakes

THERE CAN BE NO END TO A NEW BEGINNING

I hope that coming to the end of this book signals the beginning of a superb relationship with your mate, your children, and life. In a way, it's good that relationships are no longer automatically assumed to last "until death do us part." With all of the options and opportunities now open to us, we must work harder and smarter for our relationships to endure and our love to last. Love alone is no longer sufficient to keep us together. Loving actions on a daily basis are needed to strengthen our relationship into one that will last a lifetime and be rewarding and fulfilling.

Now that you know how, the rest is easy. Remember to keep your index cards with you and refer to them over and over, until the principles in this book become second nature to you. Let your knowledge lead to action as you apply the homework assignments at the end of each chapter. You will see immediate results. Acceptance, mutual support, a sense of belonging, trust, joy, and satisfaction are all possible, starting today!

Above all, keep a sense of humor when the kids are driving you crazy. The behavior that drives you crazy today will be gone tomorrow. As a matter of fact, the child who drives you crazy today will be gone someday, too. So put your energy into your relationship first—it will be with you longer than your children will.

I know that since you read this book, you are searching for "more." Just how much more you'll get will depend on how much more you are willing to give. Don't worry that by giving more to each other you will be depriving your children. In fact, the opposite is true. I can't stress enough my conviction that by concentrating on your relationship—making it the best it can be—you give your children the greatest gift of all: the opportunity to grow up in a home that is filled with love and security. Only by modeling a loving, romantic, fun-filled partnership can you pass the legacy on to your children. What greater gift could a parent provide?

Please write to me as you have in the past and let me know how you're doing. Who knows, you may be in my next book!

LHF
P.O. Box 1511
Lake Forest, CA 92630

Here's to your children and to you lighting each other's fires forever!

Love,
Ellen

ABOUT THE AUTHOR

ELLEN KREIDMAN, bestselling author and creator of *Light His Fire* and *Light Her Fire*, has a combined B.A. in psychology and education and a Ph.D. in human relations. For the past fifteen years she has been a dynamic public speaker, motivating and educating thousands of men and women. She remains passionately in love with her husband of thirty years and is the mother of three.

Marie Papillon has been hailed as *the* authority on love and romance. All over the world, men and women have learned her secrets of amour with fantastic results. Now, in her phenomenal bestselling book, she reveals:

• How, where and even when to meet that special someone—from walking the dog to working out to hosting a "blind date" party

• How to become an irresistible flirt—mastering verbal and non-verbal techniques...from making eye contact to talking on the phone to computer flirting!

• Tips for rekindling passion—from planning romantic menus for "theme evenings" to sending a bouquet of balloons and other creative ideas!

• Helpful hints for romance on a budget

• And much more!

A Million and One Love Strategies

♥ Marie Papillon ♥

A MILLION AND ONE LOVE STRATEGIES
Marie Papillon
_____ 95466-2 $5.99 U.S./$6.99 CAN.